Financing Change

Financing Change
The Financial Community,
Eco-efficiency, and
Sustainable Development

Stephan Schmidheiny and
Federico Zorraquín
with the World Business
Council for Sustainable
Development

The MIT Press
Cambridge, Massachusetts
London, England

This book was set in Palatino by Wellington Graphics.
Printed on recycled paper and bound in the United States of America.

Library of Congress Cataloging-in-Publication Data
Schmidheiny, Stephan, 1947–
  Financing change : the financial community, eco-efficiency, and sustainable development / Stephan Schmidheiny and Federico Zorraquín : with the World Business Council for Sustainable Development.
  p. cm.
  Includes bibliographical references and index.
  ISBN 0-262-19370-1 (alk. paper)
  1. Financial services industry—Environmental aspects.
2. Financial services—Moral and ethical aspects. 3. Social responsibility of business.
4. Liability for environmental damages. 5. Sustainable development. 6. Economic development—Environmental aspects. I. Zorraquín, Federico J. II. Title.
HG173.S297 1996
332.1'068'4—dc20   95-44373
                                                                        CIP

Contents

Foreword

Thirty years ago, concern for environmental issues was restricted to small groups of scientists and activists but was effectively nonexistent among the business and financial communities. Since about the time of the Stockholm environment conference in 1972, awareness of environmental problems has become more central to the thinking of innovative industrialists. This process is now gradually spreading within the financial community as banks and other financial institutions realize that they cannot ignore the implications of environmental policies and concerns for their own businesses.

As an investment banker prior to my appointment as President of the World Bank, I was closely involved with the World Business Council for Sustainable Development, and am proud to be a member. Through that connection I have observed with interest the ways in which environmental concerns have become more important to the mainstream activities of the financial sector. Thus, I welcome this valuable contribution to the debate about how businesses and financial institutions should take account of environmental issues. It puts forward many interesting ideas on the appropriate incentives to encourage commercial enterprises to take account of the environment and the need for sustainable development in their day-to-day operations.

At the World Bank we regard the promotion of environmentally sustainable development as one of our fundamental objectives. Thus, we look forward to building upon the ideas and approaches outlined in this book as well as to cooperating with the business and financial communities in promoting the wide adoption of the most effective practical measures that are emerging from the current debate. At the same time, we recognize that the achievement of sound environmental practices depends upon a constructive partnership between businesses and governments. We hope that we can play a useful role in promoting such partnerships and in assisting governments to put in place incentives that ensure that economic growth is sustainable.

James D. Wolfensohn
President
The World Bank

Acknowledgments

Since work on this issue began in 1993, the Business Council for Sustainable Development (BCSD) and, as from the beginning of 1995, the World Business Council for Sustainable Development (WBCSD) have received advice, counsel, and information from many people and organizations both inside and outside the Working Group established to work on the issue.

We are deeply indebted to all who have contributed to and supported our work, and regret that we cannot list them all here.

Given that many facts in the book came directly from members of the task force or outside experts, it has been difficult to source every assertion in the book. Despite the many people involved, the opinions expressed in this book remain the sole responsibility of the authors.

WBCSD Working Group
(*denotes members of the editing group)

Chairs

*Stephan Schmidheiny, Chairman Anova Holding AG
*Federico Zorraquín, President of the Group S.A. Garovaglio y Zorraquín

Members

*Rick J. Anderson, Noranda Inc., Toronto
*Richard Blundell, SGS Société Général de Surveillance, Geneva

*Frank W. Bosshardt, Anova Holding AG, Hurden, Switzerland

Prof. Dr. Arie F. Brand, SHV Holdings N.V., Utrecht, The Netherlands

Jeri Eagan, Shell International Petroleum Company Limited, London

Michael Federmann, Dan Hotels Corporation Ltd., Tel-Aviv

Dr. Raymond Florin, Consejo Empresario Argentino Para El Desarrollo Sostenible, Buenos Aires

Dr. Jeffrey A. Goldstein, James D. Wolfensohn, Inc., New York

Petr Horacek, Czech BCSD, Prague

Carlos Joly, UNI Storebrand, Oslo

*Franz A. Knecht, Swiss Bank Corporation, Basle, Switzerland

Johannes Lehmann, Volkswagen AG, Wolfburg, Germany

Ginés Navarro, Fundación Juan March, Madrid

Catharina Nystedt-Ringborg, ABB Asea Brown Boveri Ltd., Stockholm, Sweden

Dr. Sylvia Adriana Pinal Calvillo, BCSD Latin America, Monterrey, Mexico

*Dr. Friedrich J. Sauerländer, SGS Société Générale de Surveillance S.A., Geneva

Dr. L.-G. Scheidt, Sony Europa GmbH, Fellbach, Germany

Sir Colin Southgate, THORN EMI plc, London

Dr. W. Ross Stevens III , DuPont, Wilmington, Delaware, USA

*Björn Stigson, WBCSD, Geneva

*Hilary Thompson, National Westminster Bank, London

Wallace M. Vrooman, Avenor Inc., Ottawa

*Peter Zollinger, Anova Holding AG, Hurden, Switzerland

External Panel of Experts

Andreas Bürge, Arthur Andersen AG, Zürich

Jeremy Eppel, Environment Directorate, OECD, Paris

John Graham, EDI World Institute, Montreal

Heinrich Greiner, Münchener Rückversicherungs-Gesellschaft, Munich

Marilyn G. Haft, Green Audit, Inc., New York

Dr. Hazel Henderson, Alternative World Futures, Inc., St. Augustine, Florida

Henriette Hindrichsen, Norwegian School of Management, Oslo

Paul Holden, World Bank, Washington

Inge Kaul, Office of Development Studies, UNDP, New York

David Lascelles, Financial Times, London

Mark Mansley, Delphi International, London

*Eric Ohlund, Arthur Andersen AG, Zürich

*Nicholas Parker, Delphi International, London

Robert H. Ray, Moody's Investors Service, New York

Dr. Michael Rubino, International Finance Corporation, Washington

Richard L. Sandor, Centre Financial Products Limited, New York

Stefan Schaltegger, WWZ Universität Basel, Basel, Switzerland

Joseph Tanega, Kingston Business School, London

Tessa Tennant, NPI, London

Richard P. Turrin, AIG Risk Management, New York

Scott Vaughan, United Nations Environment Programme, Geneva

Eckardt Wintzen, BSO/Origin, Utrecht, The Netherlands

Donna Wise, World Resources Institute, Washington

Sponsors

We are especially grateful for the support of Arthur Andersen AG, Zürich, the main financial sponsor of this work in addition to the WBCSD. Arthur Andersen intends to organize seminars on the findings of the book in several financial centers around the world. We are also grateful for the financial support of Sulzer Brothers, Winterthur, Switzerland.

Although it is extremely difficult to single out anyone, we would like to thank in particular a few individuals who were helpful in providing original material: David Lascelles, Mark Mansley, Nicholas Parker, Robert H. Ray, Dr. Michael Rubino, Richard L. Sandor, Dr. Friedrich J. Sauerländer, Joseph Tanega, Tessa Tennant, Hilary Thompson, Richard P. Turrin, and Scott Vaughan.

A team from the Basel-based consulting firm Ellipson AG, led by Kaspar Müller and aided by Andreas Sturm and Anja Wittke, did much of the basic research.

This material was subsequently reviewed by the WBCSD Working Group, assisted by the panel of experts from outside the WBCSD. The research was gradually forged into the present book by Lloyd Timberlake, assisted by Peter Knight, Shelly Fennell, and Linda Starke.

World Business Council
  for Sustainable Development
160, Route de Florissant
CH-1231, Conches-Geneva
Switzerland
Tel: 41 (22) 839-3100
Fax: 41 (22) 839-3131

The World Business Council for Sustainable Development (WBCSD)

The WBCSD was formed in January 1995 through a merger between the Business Council for Sustainable Development (BCSD) in Geneva and the World Industry Council for the Environment (WICE) in Paris—the two organizations that led the business response to the challenges arising from the United Nations Conference on Environment and Development in Rio in 1992.

With more than 120 members in 35 countries representing more than 20 major industrial sectors, the WBCSD is a powerful business voice on sustainable development issues—and plays an important role in developing closer cooperation between business, government, and others, and in encouraging high standards of environmental and resource management in business itself. Its mission is to provide business leadership as a catalyst for change toward sustainable development, and to promote eco-efficiency in business.

Its objectives are to be the leading business advocate for issues regarding sustainable development; to participate in policy development to create the right framework conditions for business to make an effective contribution toward sustainable development; to demonstrate progress in eco-efficiency in business and to share leading edge practices among members; and to contribute to a sustainable future for developing nations and nations in transition.

WBCSD reports, such as this book, are released in the name of the WBCSD and the Working Group chairs, after having been reviewed in summary form by the Liaison Delegates of Council members and submitted in summary form to the Executive Committee for final approval. Thus not every member necessarily agrees with every word in any report, and the opinions expressed therein remain those of the named authors.

WBCSD Members

1. Western Europe

Denmark
Danfoss A/S
dk-Teknik
Novo Nordisk A/S

Finland
Kymmene Corporation
Neste Oy
Pohjolan Voima Oy

France
Clifford Chance
Deloitte Touche Tohmatsu International
Lafarge
Renault SA
Rhône Poulenc
Total S.A.

Germany
Gerling Konzern Insurances
Henkel KGaA
Lurgi AG (Metallgesellschaft Group)
Volkswagen AG

Italy
Fiat Auto S.p.A.
Pirelli S.p.A.

The Netherlands
Akzo Nobel n.v.
Heineken N.V.
Philips Electronics N.V.
SHV Holdings N.V.
Unilever N.V.

Norway
Kværner a.s.
Norsk Hydro A.S.
Orkla A.S.

Saga Petroleum a.s.
Statoil
UNI Storebrand A.S.

Portugal
Sonae Investimentos S.G.P.S., S.A.

Spain
Fundación Juan March

Sweden
ABB Asea Brown Boveri Ltd.
AB Volvo
Axel Johnson Group
Stora
Tetra Laval Group

Switzerland
Anova Holding AG
Ciba-Geigy AG
F. Hofmann-La Roche Ltd.
Nestlé Ltd.
Sandoz International Ltd.
Schindler Holding SA
SGS Société Générale de Surveillance Holding S.A.
Sulzer Ltd.
Swiss Bank Corporation

Turkey
Dogus Holding A.S.
Koç Holding A.S.

United Kingdom
The BOC Group plc
British Gas plc
The British Petroleum Company plc
The Environmental Resources Management Group
Glaxo Wellcome plc
Grand Metropolitan plc
Imperial Chemical Industries plc
John Laing plc
National Westminster Bank plc

PowerGen plc
The RTZ Corporation plc
Shell International Petroleum Company Limited
THORN EMI plc
Waste Management International plc

2. Central – Eastern Europe

Czech Republic
Chemical Works Sokolov, JSC
Poland
Investment Consortium

3. Africa – Middle East

Cameroon
Compagnie Financière et Industrielle S.A.
Israel
Dan Hotels Corporation Ltd.
Nigeria
BEWAC plc
South Africa
ESKOM
Zimbabwe
Delta Corporation Limited

4. North America

Canada
Avenor Inc.
Noranda Inc.
Northern Telecom Limited
Ontario Hydro
TransAlta Corporation
United States
AT&T
The Dow Chemical Company
DuPont Company Inc.

Interface, Inc.
International Paper Company
James D. Wolfensohn Inc.
Johnson & Johnson
Monsanto Company
S.C. Johnson & Son, Inc.
The Procter & Gamble Company
3M Company
Texaco Inc.
Weyerhaeuser
Xerox Corporation

5. Latin America

Argentina
S.A. Garovaglio y Zorraquín
Brazil
Aracruz Celulose S.A.
Caemi Mineração e Metalurgia S.A.
Rio Doce International SA
Chile
CAP S.A.
Colombia
De Lima & Cia Ltda
Mexico
Aeromexico
Exincomer, S.A. de C.V.
Grupo IMSA, S.A. de C.V.
Laboratorios Columbia, SA de C.V.

6. Japan

Hitachi Ltd.
International Development Center of Japan
Itochu Corporation
Kajima Corporation
The KANSAI Electric Power Co., Inc.
Kikkoman Corporation

Mitsubishi Corporation
Mitsui & Co. Ltd.
Nippon Telegraph and Telephone Corporation
NEC Corporation
Osaka Gas Co. Ltd.
Seiko Group
Sony Corporation
The Tokyo Electric Power Company Inc.
Tokyo Gas Company Ltd.
Toray Industries Inc.
Toshiba Corporation
Toyota Motor Corporation
The Yasuda Fire & Marine Insurance Company Limited

7. Asia

India
CESC Limited
Indonesia
Indonesian Wood Panel Association
Korea
Samsung Electronics
Taiwan
Taiwan Cement Corporation
Thailand
Thai Farmers Bank

8. Oceania

Australia
Western Mining Corporation Ltd.
New Zealand
Fletcher Challenge Limited
Heinz-Wattie Limited

Executive Summary

In this book we pose a question, attempt an answer, and in the process make tentative proposals on how financial markets could begin to support the goals of eco-efficiency and sustainable development.

The Question

Are the world's financial markets and those who work in and around them a force for sustainable human progress, or are they an impediment against it?

This question recognizes the critical role played by financial markets in the way we organize our commercial, industrial, and personal lives. It acknowledges that any form of development—sustainable or not— must be financed largely by these markets.

There is sufficient evidence to support the view that many of our current activities are not sustainable in the long term and that they stifle opportunity for a sizable proportion of the world's fast-expanding population.

This realization leads to two further, fundamental questions: Do the financial markets encourage a short-termist, profits-only mentality that ignores much human and environmental reality? Or are they simply tools that reflect human concerns, and so will eventually reflect disquiet over poverty and the degradation of nature by rewarding companies that treat people and the environment in a responsible manner?

The Answer

Although the question is succinct, the response is inevitably more complex. In an attempt to find answers, we examine both the workings of the financial markets—established and emerging—and the roles of different key players in the financial community.

We look at how these players are responding to environmental demands on their professions. The findings are mixed, but we detect enough encouraging activity to refute in part the received wisdom that the financial community is, at best, ignorant of the idea of sustainable development or, at worst, dismissive of it.

Not only are the players more aware of the issues than their critics claim, but many of them are grappling with the complexities of the debate. Some, like insurers, if only for reasons of self-preservation, are beginning to take steps to guarantee that their activities contribute to rather than hamper progress toward a sustainable future.

Company leaders—chief executives, board-level directors, and owners—have been the first to feel the effects of environmental change. Consequently, most large concerns have become more eco-efficient—that is, they add ever more value while using fewer resources and producing less pollution. Because of their broad level of responsibility, company leaders have had to understand and accommodate the sometimes contradictory needs of their key stakeholders and then forge strong relationships with them. We find that those who run small and medium-sized businesses need to catch up fast, however.

We urge company leaders to build a sustainable development reflex into corporate activities, so that when the markets come to reward eco-efficiency more systematically, company leaders will have their strategies in place, their teams trained and fit, and their stakeholders loyal.

Mainstream **investors** in equities (stocks or shares) largely dismiss environmental concerns because they are seen as moral issues outside their realm. Those in the financial community who are contracted to manage funds for others point to their legal duty to maximize returns on investments without reference to the morality of environmental damage or social justice.

Even so, we find evidence of change. Investors are beginning to look at the environmental costs and potential environmental liabilities of companies and how these affect share performance. A small but vocal minority of investors and their agents are beginning to broaden their interpretation of fiduciary duty. Some are beginning to question the nineteenth-century definition of prudence and are looking for ways to incorporate society's current concerns. Already, some pension funds are allocating small sums to be invested in socially important but financially risky projects. And so-called ethical investors are using their position in the markets to create a dialogue with company management on the importance of eco-efficiency.

Ways must be found to help markets better understand the environment, probably by putting a price on it. This can be achieved by policies that emphasize market mechanisms, such as tradable emissions certificates. More broadly, and in the interests of efficient markets, "owners" of capital who are now remote from the workings of their capital—such as pensioners and shareholders—should be supplied with the necessary information so that they can influence those who make decisions on their behalf.

Bankers know that under certain circumstances they can be held responsible by society, through the legal system, for the environmental wrongs of their borrowers. To limit their risk, bankers are beginning to consider eco-efficiency in their lending decisions, on the assumption that companies with a bad environmental performance pose a high financial risk. They are beginning to understand that a company's creditworthiness depends more and more on its eco-efficiency.

Leading banks have largely mitigated their own environmental risk exposure, but we suggest that bankers now look more closely for opportunities to provide financial products and services that help others reduce their risks too.

Insurers have already suffered direct financial damage from environmental problems. Claims against general liability policies for damages from asbestos exposure and hazardous waste dumping in the United States are estimated to cost the insurance industry $2 trillion. Now insurers are worried about the possibility of climate change and how this could, in the future, damage their business. Some in the industry argue that insurers should recognize that their interests are different from those who sell carbon fuel or use it in large quantities— the so-called carbon club. One view now gaining support in the industry is that insurers should lobby for policies that reduce the risks of climate change.

We recommend that the insurance industry use its experience with hazardous waste as a model for how to deal with the threat of climate change. At the very least, this industry should recognize that its interests are different from those of the more vocal and politically astute in heavy industry.

Accountants know that many of their colleagues in the financial community are looking to them to devise systems that put numbers to environmental risks and opportunities. Auditors, especially, are aware of their role in verifying that company accounts truly reflect a company's viability in a changing world. But accountants are caught in a difficult position. They can play only according to the rules of the game, which exclude most environmental concerns. They realize, too, that it is their job to find a way of valuing what society values—and this means putting a price on those things that are now considered external to the accounts, such as damage to common resources.

Some on the academic side of the accounting profession are highly articulate on sustainability and have already provided sound ideas on how the profession can accommodate this concept. Some practitioners, especially those advising companies involved in mergers and acquisitions, have been quick to identify environmental risks that devalue companies, and these decisions have been reflected in the markets.

We suggest that accountants strive to help eco-efficient companies communicate their progress (and the business benefits) to the markets, and then help the markets understand the benefits so that they can bestow the necessary rewards.

Accountants could be helped by **raters**—those who judge the creditworthiness of companies and countries, and who are slowly beginning to include environmental issues in their judging process. Their slow progress has provided an opportunity for others who have been experimenting with ways to put a price on the environment, and with how to make life easier for their colleagues in the financial community who might need that information.

We see opportunity for eco-efficient companies to communicate their progress to the markets through ratings. We think it probable that traditional ratings agencies will make even greater efforts to reflect environmental risk in their products. We urge them to identify opportunities too.

Our society and its financial markets are caught between the short-term tendencies of individuals and civilization's longer-term need to sustain itself. Society must take a longer view and create the necessary frameworks to reward businesses for adding ever more value while using fewer resources and producing less pollution. Only then can society expect the markets to support sustainable development.

I   The Game

1   Eco-efficiency and the Financial Markets

Will financial markets soon be systematically rewarding environmentally successful companies while penalising offenders? Some serious people think so.

—*Institutional Investor,*
March 1995

This book addresses a burning question that almost no one seems to be asking: Are the workings of the world's financial markets—stocks, bonds, debt, currency instruments—and the financial community a force for sustainable human progress, or are they an impediment against it?

In other words, do the financial markets encourage a short-termist, profits-only mentality that ignores much human and environmental reality? Or are they simply tools that reflect human concerns, and so will eventually reflect concerns over poverty and the degradation of nature by rewarding firms and projects that increase equity of opportunity and that rationally manage environmental resources?

These are crucial questions. The world stock market capitalization (the sum of all stock markets) at the end of 1994 totalled more than $15 trillion ($15,000 billion)—more than 2.5 times the gross national product (GNP) of the United States.[1] The world bond market at the end of 1993 held more than $16 trillion in publicly issued debt.[2] It is a little frightening not knowing whether such vast sums are working for or against sustainable progress.

There are several other closely related reasons why these questions need early answers.

First, the world's population is growing rapidly and may double to more than 11 billion sometime next century unless serious measures

Chapter 1 Summary

Do the financial markets support sustainable development—forms of development that allow people today and in the future to meet their needs? There are reasons to believe they do not, in that they may encourage short-term goals, undervalue environmental resources, discount the future, and favor accounting and reporting systems that do not reflect environmental risks and opportunities.

The issue is pressing because investment decisions being taken now set the paths of development for the next few decades, when human populations will increase rapidly and billions of people will enter market economies.

Businesses that use and sell natural resources and cause pollution have grappled with environment and sustainable development issues longer than have companies dealing in shares, banking, and insurance. They have developed the concept of eco-efficiency: increasing value added while decreasing pollution and resource use.

All businesses are facing changes in the marketplace: the polluter pays principle, which will force the cost of a company's environmental damage onto the company books; greater use of economic instruments, which reward the eco-efficient and punish their lagging competitors; and possible changes in tax structures and national accounting systems.

As these trends change the bottom lines of companies, financial markets will change the ways in which they value them. The financial community will start rewarding eco-efficiency for purely financial reasons.

are taken to slow the increase.[3] And there are roughly 1 billion very poor people on the planet today.[4] The concept of sustainable human progress has come to be summed up in the ideal of "sustainable development," best defined as a style of progress or development that "meets the needs of the present without compromising the ability of future generations to meet their own needs."[5]

Obviously, economic "no growth" is not an option if the needs of the present poor or of future, larger, generations are to be met. The World Commission on Environment and Development (WCED) argued that sustainable development does imply limits—"not absolute limits but limitation imposed by the present state of technology and social organization."[6] Growth, then, will have to be extremely "eco-efficient," a term the Business Council for Sustainable Development (BCSD) coined to describe a process of adding ever more value while steadily decreasing resource use, waste, and pollution.[7]

Second, major investments are being made now that will determine the sustainability of today's economic growth: investments in energy, transport, agricultural, water, and sewage systems. Asia (excluding Japan)—perhaps the fastest growing "developing" region on earth—needs to invest about $1 trillion ($1,000 billion) in its infrastructure between 1994 and 2004, with about 70 percent of this total being power- and transport-related, according to an estimate by Standard & Poor's.[8] Much of this capital must come from the financial markets: the equity markets, bond markets, and the banks. But will these investments reflect environmental realities? To take one example, coal has traditionally offered the lowest costs for generating electricity. Yet burning coal also emits a large amount of carbon dioxide (CO_2). A great many of the power plants being planned and financed in Asia are traditional coal ones at a time when the governments of the world have agreed to stabilize their CO_2 emissions at 1990 levels by the year 2000.

Third, sustainable development means passing along to future generations certain stocks of environmental capital: productive topsoil, clean air, predictable climate, an intact ozone layer, fertile forests, abundant fish stocks, and genetic diversity of both plants and animals. Scientists warn that all these resources are under threat by the activities of the present generation. Again, to cite but one example, over the past century the extinction rates among plant and animals species have risen to 100 to 1,000 times "natural" or "background" rates.[9] These human-caused extinction rates are expected to accelerate, even without global warming. What, if anything, can the financial community do to reverse such trends?

Fourth, more than 3 billion people in Eastern Europe, Asia, and Latin America are changing from more or less centrally planned economies to market economies. If economic growth continues to follow patterns predicted by the World Bank for the coming decade, by the year 2020 the present "rich world" share of global output could shrink to less than 40 percent from more than 55 percent today, measured in terms of purchasing power parities.[10] By then, China, India, Indonesia,

Brazil, and Mexico will be on the list of the world's 15 biggest economies. All are countries with high population growth rates; in all,
natural resources are already under great pressure. In a warning that
could apply to several other rapidly developing nations, the World
Bank reported to Indonesia in 1994 that growing pollution and con-
gestion in its main urban centers could make it "increasingly difficult
for Indonesia to compete for foreign investment, especially in the
higher technology industries needed to enhance the productivity of the
labor force."[11] How can these countries see to it that the financial
markets back projects that favor sustainable, long-term progress rather
than a "get-rich-quick" approach?

Fifth, "socialism" appears to be dead. The "market" is taking over as
the determiner of the direction of investments. Markets are being
deregulated; they are becoming global, which severely limits the ability of individual governments to control them; and goods and services
once provided by governments are being privatized. Private investment has taken over from "foreign aid" as the main mover of capital
into the developing world. Let us look at some figures.

Flows of private capital to developing countries quadrupled between 1986 and 1994, by which point they had reached more than $170
billion a year, according to the World Bank.[12] This included such things
as foreign direct investment (such as investment by foreign companies
into joint ventures), private debt (such as loans by commercial banks
or proceeds from the sale of bonds internationally), and portfolio
equity investment (such as purchases of shares by pension funds or
mutual funds).

The Organisation for Economic Co-operation and Development
(OECD) put the 1994 flow of official development assistance (ODA)
from members of its Development Assistance Committee (most of the
world's aid-giving countries) at $57.3 billion.[13] For the fourth consecu-
tive year, private flows rose and official flows fell in real terms. These
trends are expected to continue. An international group of development charities reported in 1995 that ODA that year represented a
smaller proportion of wealthy nations' GNPs than at any time over the
past 20 years.[14] Should the U.S. government follow through on some
U.S. lawmakers' efforts to slash its aid budget, the decline would
accelerate sharply. Given that other countries, such as Canada, are

threatening to follow the U.S. lead, "foreign aid" as traditionally practiced may be virtually over.

Governments, both donor and recipient, have never really managed to make aid flows environmentally sound. But at least with these government-to-government transfers it is clear that this responsibility lies with governments. How are the environmental quality and sustainability content of the new private investment flows to be assured? This is an important issue because, according to Brad Gentry at Yale University's Center for Environmental Law and Policy, "these private investments are often made in projects with immediate environmental implications, such as: privatizations of government-owned manufacturing enterprises; concessions to private developers of power, water, transportation and other infrastructure facilities; joint ventures for the operation of existing or the construction of new manufacturing plants; as well as energy and natural resource projects."[15] Thus if the market is taking over from governments as the coordinator of human progress, it is crucial that the market tend toward sustainability.

There are even those who argue that the increasing power of financial markets is actually threatening the power of national governments. According to British journalist Hamish McRae:

The rise of the power of the financial markets, together with their increasingly international nature, has inevitably reduced the power of the individual national governments. They have to frame their economic policies with an eye to the way these will be received by the world's financial community. If they fail to do so, they will be punished by either a run on the currency or higher interest rates, or both.[16]

Seven Key Assumptions

To some readers, worrying about how the financial community can support sustainable development will seem as farfetched as wondering how stock market results can help them pick horse race winners. But as we make clear in part II, such work is already being done within all sectors of that community. Our purpose is largely to report the current efforts of market players.

But first we want to set out some thoughts on how difficult such work can be. There are seven suppositions that helped us think about the questions asked in the preceding section. We do not offer these as truths, or even as strong beliefs, but as assumptions that emerged in our discussions with experts as we researched this book. Taken together, they are worrying, and suggest how much change will be required before financial markets encourage, rather than discourage, sustainable development.

• Sustainable development requires investments with long payback. Financial markets seek short-term payback.

• Efforts toward eco-efficiency by a company often reduce present earnings in favor of future potentials. Financial markets favor companies with high present earnings over those with future potentials.

• Given low resource prices and the ability of businesses to keep costs for much environmental damage "external" to their own balance sheets, the profitability of becoming eco-efficient is reduced. Eco-efficient companies are often not preferred by financial markets.

• Sustainable development requires massive investments in developing countries. Financial markets put a high risk premium on investments in developing countries.

• High taxes on employment encourage labor productivity, thereby enhancing unemployment, while low resource prices discourage resource efficiency.

• Accounting and reporting systems do not adequately convey potential environmental risks or opportunities. Financial markets are compelled to make decisions based on biased information.

• Sustainable development is concerned with the importance of the future. Financial markets discount the future routinely and heavily.

We shall be dealing with these assumptions at various places in subsequent chapters, and return to them specifically in part III, The Scorecard.

No discussion of the relationships between markets and sustainability would be complete without reference to some academic work that seems to suggest that markets virtually always work against sustainability. In 1976, Colin Clark's *Mathematical Bioeconomics: The Optimal Management of Renewable Resources* was published as a volume in a series on pure and applied mathematics.[17] Clark was particularly concerned with the concept of maximum sustainable yield (MSY). This is the highest number of trees, fish, nuts, or any other renewable resource that can be harvested year after year. If you harvest any more, the resource cannot produce such a high annual "surplus." But harvest any less and you are below the maximum. The MSY is essentially the highest "interest" to be gained from a renewable resource.

Clark has a great deal to say about the limits of the MSY approach, but he offers a hypothetical case early on. Assume there are 75,000 blue whales in the oceans, and that the MSY is 2,000 whales per year. Imagine for simplicity's sake that only one company can hunt this stock, and that each processed whale has a market value of $10,000. By whaling sustainably—2,000 whales a year—the company would produce an annual revenue of $20 million.

Now assume that it is possible for the company to catch all 75,000 whales in a single year, producing a lump sum revenue of $750 million. If this were invested at a modest rate of return of 5 percent a year, it would yield an annual return of $35.7 million, considerably above the $20 million figure and without the inconvenience of whaling. Although this is a simplistic model, in 350 pages of highly mathematical discussions of the complexities of market elasticity, discount rates, and so on, Clark shows that the basic findings remain the same for most renewable resources.

Basically, the profitability of harvesting a renewable resource rarely encourages sustainable harvesting; it stimulates the opposite, even where there is a single owner and no poorly controlled competition, as in most fisheries today. To make matters worse, the MSY of long-lived, slow-reproducing species such as whales or tropical hardwoods is very low, on the order of 2 percent. Only short-lived, fast-reproducing species such as shrimp have an MSY beginning to equal market interest rates. The large unpredictable fluctuations of some stocks, such as many fish species, also encourage exploitation sooner rather than later.

"The argument illustrates one of the fundamental aspects of the economics of resource management," Clark wrote. "The owner of a resource stock tends to view that stock as a *capital asset;* this is equally true for exhaustible resources and for renewable resources. He expects the asset to earn dividends at the 'normal' rate of return; otherwise, the owner would attempt to dispose of the asset." He adds that this result may be thought of as "the first fundamental theorem of resource economics," and was developed as early as 1931.

Today this syndrome is best seen in the activities of many international logging companies, which acquire from governments the rights to log natural forests at prices far below any reasonable market rates. One study of this phenomenon found that although obligations to reforest presented liabilities, they rarely appeared on balance sheets, and in fact frequently the obligations were ignored.[18] Given the companies' windfall profits and few announced liabilities, their shares have performed extremely well over the past few years. It is not clear whether the shareholders understand the unsustainable nature of the companies' activities—from both a profitability and an ecological point of view—and are poised to sell out before windfall profits cease. But it is clear that the globalization of investment flows is speeding the destruction of natural forests.

Business and the Environment

Yet the picture may not be as bleak as we have suggested. Although concern about the relationships between the financial markets and sustainable development is still very much in its infancy, it is growing. Even more important, a number of business leaders, investors, analysts, bankers, insurers, accountants, and raters have moved beyond a focus solely on downside risk toward one of taking advantage of upside opportunities. In each sector, a few actors are making a good business out of society's search for sustainability.

In the rest of this chapter we examine how these sustainability issues got onto the agendas of business in general and of the financial community in particular. To do so, we must look at how the business view of "the environment" has changed rapidly over the past decade.

Until fairly recently, the environment was discussed as something separate from human activities except where those activities damaged it. A small minority—often referred to as environmentalists—were deeply worried over that damage; the vast majority were not. Businesses' concern for the environment expressed itself through efforts to comply with environmental regulations and to lobby against them.

During the eighties, increasing evidence of global carbon pollution, ozone depletion, and the loss of species, forests, and fertile soils suggested that environmental damage was more global and more serious than previously expected. It also became clear that the environment was not a place outside of the human sphere but rather a set of processes affected by all human activities: business, manufacturing, consuming, farming, fishing, mining, and so on. Thus the old battle between those championing the environment and those advocating "development" began to die down slightly when the two goals were seen more and more as inseparable sides of the same coin. It became harder to worry about the natural environment and not be concerned about people's needs and aspirations. It also became harder to worry about people and not be concerned about their impact on the natural environment.

This new view was best encapsulated in the concept of sustainable development. Since the modern form of the concept (an idea as old, in fact, as the earliest hunter-gatherer societies) emerged in the mid-eighties, there have been many books written and organizations established on sustainable development. There is broad agreement that it is not a goal restricted to "developing" countries. All nations are developing in the dictionary sense of "evolving the possibilities of," and many industrial nations are evolving their possibilities in ways that make the planet less sustainable, both because of consumption patterns there and because of their release of global pollutants.

Yet the concept remains ill defined. It is much more obvious in the negative than the positive. Present rates of population growth appear unsustainable, but it is less clear what a sustainable human population might be. We may be burning too much coal, oil, and gas for the climate's sake, but it is not clear precisely what a sustainable energy path might be.

Imprecise as it is, the concept is very powerful. People instinctively feel that the first duty of parents is to provide for their children. Unsustainable development is the opposite; it means that the present generation takes resources away from future generations. It is stealing from our children.

The idea of sustainable development has been an effective force in bringing new groups into debates about progress and the environment. A growing number of economists are busy defining sustainability in economic terms. Jurists are wrestling with the legal basis for equity between this generation and those to come. Some politicians worry about how the craft of politics can be made to peer beyond the next election to concern itself with the needs of our progeny.

Business has been slow to come to terms with sustainable development, partly due to a traditional resistance toward organized forms of environmental concerns and partly due to an inability to see what business has to do with the non-market needs of people today or the necessities of people in the future, who do not participate in today's markets.

But business is beginning to take an interest in these issues. The journal *Tomorrow* recently listed 40 organizations bringing businesses together for environmental and sustainable development purposes. It even gave these bodies their own acronym: GBN (Green Business Network).[19] Business is also taking part in many organizations that combine leaders from the corporate world with those from politics, science, and other non-business groups; examples of these include the (U.S.) President's Council on Sustainable Development and the Round Tables on the Environment and the Economy in Canada.

Business has made progress in grappling with these issues along what can be seen, with hindsight, as a predictable path. First came the more progressive companies in sectors with the most obvious environment/development concerns: multinational chemical and energy companies and the big manufacturers. Retailers got involved next, largely in response to "green consumerism." Then big service companies realized that they were not immune, given their use of energy, paper, and transport.

In the financial community, there had long been a few "green investment" services offering portfolios containing the shares of companies not associated with excessive pollution or misuse of environmental resources. But the first mainstream concern in the sector came from insurance companies being hit by cleanup costs for contaminated industrial sites and by costs of damage from what seemed to be an alarming rise in weather-related natural disasters. (See chapter 6.)

Most banks resisted engagement in the issue, arguing that they use virtually no natural resources and emit little pollution. When the BCSD first started looking for members in 1990, it could not find a single banker in the industrial world willing to join. (In 1995, the BCSD merged with the World Industry Council for the Environment (WICE) to become the World Business Council for Sustainable Development—the WBCSD. It is affiliated with all national BCSDs.)

Since then, however, a series of U.S. court cases suggested that banks might be held responsible for the environmental damage to industrial sites caused by companies in which the financial bodies had certain types of ownership or management functions. (See chapter 5.) These rulings concentrated the minds of the international banking community profoundly. By the beginning of the U.N. Conference on Environment and Development (the Earth Summit) in June 1992, bankers had produced, and many had signed, an international "Statement by Banks on the Environment and Sustainable Development." (See appendix.)

Just as different companies and sectors of business have been drawn into environmental concerns at different times, depending on their circumstances, so too have officers within companies. Most firms first tried to contain the environment in a special "environmental office." It soon became apparent that this was as unworkable as the political approach of creating a weak Ministry of the Environment, and then holding it responsible for the damage done by the more powerful Ministries of, for example, Transport, Industry, Mining, and Agriculture. So in progressive companies, the chief executive officer (CEO) became in practice also the chief environmental officer.

The task then became one of getting the CEO's new environmental concerns spread throughout the firm. Much has been written about this process in different companies. But it is intriguing to note that it is apparently easier to inculcate environmental thinking into the work force than into financial directors. The U.S. manufacturing company 3M is famous for drawing from its work force over the past 20 years ideas for more than 3,000 pollution-prevention projects, which have saved the company more than $500 million.[20] It is not hard to see why workers were ahead of the financial officers. Most have a daily close-up view of corporate resource waste and pollution. Once asked to consider these problems—and appropriately rewarded for doing so—they are perfectly placed to provide sound ideas.

Only much more recently have company financial officers begun to take an interest in sustainable development issues. These individuals are traditionally cut off from environmental concerns that do not get on the balance sheets. A report of the One Hundred Group of Financial Directors (the financial officers of the 100 top British companies) argued that this has been largely because of the difficulties of quantifying and measuring the costs of these risks and the costs and benefits of avoiding them.[21] But the report warned that companies lax in these matters can cause investors and banks considerable losses.

For much the same reasons, sustainable development concerns have been slow to infiltrate the financial markets. The general view is, "If we can't measure it, don't tell us about it."

Pick up any textbook on financial markets and banking and look in the index; you are unlikely to find an entry for the "environment" or "liabilities, environmental." (This was also true for the majority of business texts published before about 1990; now most of them have a lengthy list of subheadings under "environment.")

As we researched this book, we spoke to many members of financial market firms, basically asking them how they or their companies lined up in terms of environmental or sustainable development issues. The first reaction was usually surprise. This gave way to what looked a little like fear—a fear that the financial community was going to be dragged into the same messy environmental discussions and publicity that have affected other businesses.

Not only do investment banks, stockbrokerage firms, and most other financial market institutions not release toxic wastes, they do not foreclose on firms owning contaminated property and face the associated financial liabilities. Environmental risks are hard to quantify in such businesses, and it is only now becoming obvious why merchant bankers and stockbrokers should bother to look at such numbers for businesses they are considering investing in.

"We are not a major devourer of natural resources like a chemical company or a paper company," said a spokesperson for a global stockbrokerage firm, when asked if they had an environmental policy. "But we have policies on most things, so I suppose we must have an environment policy," he added. In contrast, Salomon Brothers, the investment bank, has complex programs on recycling, waste reduction, energy efficiency, environmental education, and environmental financial risk management.[22]

But most of the market participants' answers to the question of the relationship between sustainable development and the financial community can be summed up in yet another question: "Why should I care?" One purpose of this book is to offer some practical answers to that question.

One answer, but far from the most important one, is that environmental groups are now trying to achieve their goals by putting pressure on the financial community.

Some groups have protested against Initial Public Offerings on stock exchanges. In 1993, a consortium of environmental pressure groups tried to dissuade fund managers from investing in an offering of Barito Pacific, an Indonesian timber company. (See chapter 4.) After its 1994 annual meeting, Greenpeace International announced that it was going to spend more effort influencing the public and private cash flows for projects that affect the environment.[23] The organization did not make clear how it intended to do this, but earlier that year it had started issuing press releases and writing to investment companies when it saw a market event that it considered harmful.

In October 1994, for example, Greenpeace warned European fund managers about plans to float a polyvinyl chloride company, European Vinyls Corporation (EVC), on the Amsterdam stock exchange. The group, which has campaigned against the use of chlorine, argued that "environmental concerns are fundamental to EVC's market prospects and profitability and that ignoring these concerns could be ruinous for investors and the company itself." Thus when it involves itself in the markets, Greenpeace wisely emphasizes financial damage rather than environmental damage. The group has also organized several meetings with insurers, bankers, and other financial people, mainly to warn them about investments that could accelerate climate change.

"And of course we still have our in-the-street confrontational tactics," said a Greenpeace representative. "The commercial banks, which rely on the general public for business, would be deeply embarrassed by that sort of bad publicity." (We quote Greenpeace a number of times in this book, not because we necessarily agree with them, but because they have been by far the most sophisticated green group in trying to get their issues onto the agenda of the financial community.)

When Michael Heseltine was president of Britain's Board of Trade, he told the British financial community in a 1992 lecture: "Sooner or later, even the most naive environmentalist is going to grasp the extent to which companies, who are their most accustomed targets, operate within a context set by shareholders, lenders and insurers. At that time, the green searchlight will be turned directly on the way in which you discharge your environmental responsibilities."[24]

Thus for various reasons, commercial banks, investment banks, insurers, and others in the financial community who are apparently far from the front lines of environmentalism are now being drawn into the fray. But how far can businesses go in promoting sustainable development and still be acting as businesses?

Eco-efficiency Versus Sustainability

Business has only a relatively narrow band in which to modify its environment-affecting activities. Too little action, and a company may not be complying with regulations. But too much action, and it may be spending money in ways that weaken its competitiveness. Many companies that are driven more by values than by strict profit considerations will go ahead and spend some of that money to move "beyond compliance." But there are tight limits, even for such companies; a business that does not make money soon ceases to be a business.

Thus most of the impetus for progress toward sustainable development must come from voters, the governments they elect, consumers, parents, and citizens' groups. All of these will have to cooperate to build a new societal framework in which business will act.

When the BCSD was formed to offer the 1992 Earth Summit a "business perspective," it faced the problem of finding something to say that made sense in terms of environment and development but that also honored the basic realities of the marketplace. Thus the 50 original members, all CEOs or equivalent, spent much of their report to the Rio conference advising governments on which policies and rules of the game needed changing.[25]

It also held a contest to come up with a phrase that most neatly summed up the idea of sustainable development at the company level.

The winner was "eco-efficiency," which denotes both economic and ecological efficiency. According to the World Commission on Environment and Development, sustainable development "is not a fixed state of harmony, but rather a process of change in which the exploitation of resources, the direction of investments, the orientation of technological development, and institutional change are made consistent with future as well as present needs."[26] Much the same could be said for eco-efficiency: it is not a fixed state of harmony, but rather a process of change in which the exploitation of resources, the direction of investments, the orientation of technological development, and corporate change maximize value-added while minimizing resource consumption, waste, and pollution.

But eco-efficiency should not be confused with sustainable development, which is a goal for society as a whole. Though it may also require some encouragement from society in setting frameworks, eco-efficiency is a task for each entity within society. It is even possible to have a world in which every company was becoming ever more eco-efficient and yet the planet's resource base was deteriorating due to population growth and the sheer increase in business and industry.

Virtually all companies cause pollution, if only through their energy use. The U.N. Conference on Trade and Development (UNCTAD) proposed a strict definition of a "sustainable business": one that "leaves the environment no worse off at the end of each accounting period than it was at the beginning of that accounting period."[27] It then offered the obvious conclusion: "It is perfectly clear that few, if any, businesses, especially in the developed economies, come anywhere near to anything that looks remotely like sustainability."

It went on to quote a number of multinational corporations that had come to grips with this fact. The Body Shop, a cosmetics company that trades on its green image, wrote, for example: "We challenge the notion that any business can be 'environmentally friendly'. This is just not possible. All businesses involve some environmental damage. The best we can do is clear up our own mess while searching hard for ways to reduce our impact on the environment."

UNCTAD had conducted a survey in 1994 among multinational firms on their views of sustainable development; the results were based on responses from 73 companies in 14 countries, mostly in Europe, but including South Africa, South Korea, Hong Kong, and Japan. The questionnaires were filled out by the officers most knowledgeable about environmental issues, usually the senior environmental managers. The results were extremely contradictory.

Eighty-two percent of the respondents said that their companies formally recognized sustainability; yet the majority of these "formal recognitions" did not define sustainability. Ninety-six percent thought it required a partnership approach among government, business, and society; 86 percent believed it meant tackling both social and environmental problems; and 82 percent found it compatible with the profit ethic. However, 59 percent believed that sustainability did not involve the needs of future generations; 45 percent said it was synonymous with environmental management systems; and 37 percent felt that their organizations had already achieved sustainability.

So although most companies state formally that sustainability is a "Good Thing," there is some confusion over what it actually entails.

"Over 70 per cent of respondents were influenced by, *inter alia*, the ICC [International Chamber of Commerce], Agenda 21 [the summary statement of the 1992 U.N. Conference on Environment and Development] and the Rio Summit, their own company, books and economic journal articles, the media, the Brundtland [WCED] report, their national government, and professional or trade associations," UNCTAD reported. "Of these, easily the most influential were the first four," and environmental pressure groups were among the least influential. It also noted that the fact that the ICC's Charter for Sustainable Business does not actually mention or define sustainability "goes some way towards explaining what looks like naive understandings of the concept amongst many of the respondent businesses."

The survey also quoted, anonymously, some remarks of the respondents. The differences in views are striking; for example:

People need to get back to the old religion of making money and risking things. If industry went back to risking things, sustainable development would happen. (Italy)

The quest for economic growth, as demanded by national and international financial institutions, is the cause of much environmental and human exploitation. (United Kingdom)

Governments need to set clear, consistent, tax neutral and common sense targets for environmental performance and then give business the freedom to innovate and deliver the desired performance. This will lead to sustainability within a time frame of approximately 10–30 years . . . ultimately there will be a new generation of products that will build a sustainable future. (Switzerland)

It does not pay to be sustainable. Good housekeeping saves money, but the pursuit of sustainability is beyond good housekeeping—and can cost. (United Kingdom)

The survey suggests that although most multinationals say publicly that they work toward sustainable development, few have decided how to make it a part of corporate strategies. This is hardly surprising, as sustainable development does require concern for future generations and for needs that cannot easily be met by market transactions. These are issues that business has just as much trouble with as anyone else. So business joins scientists, jurists, political leaders, philosophers, and environmentalists in agreeing that "it is unsustainable to be unsustainable" and in having difficulty figuring out what activities are "sustainable." Some company directors—the ones who have moved "beyond compliance"—are therefore working on "good housekeeping" or eco-efficiency and calling it sustainability because that is the current word.

Beyond Environment

One of several revolutions occurring in the world today might be called the "participation revolution." The communications part of the technology revolution allows people to know instantly what is happening in the far reaches of the globe. So children in New York hear of and to some extent care about what is happening in the rain forests of Brazil. This knowledge and concern lead people to want to participate—in more or less serious or trivial ways. The "green consumer" movement is just one example of this.

Many people want to take part in what business is doing in new ways, such as influencing what companies produce as well as how they produce it and how they treat their employees and their neighbors. This can be local or global—and business may be targeted through no fault of its own. When France announced in 1995 that it was going to resume nuclear weapons testing in the South Pacific,

protesters in North America, Europe, and Australasia organized boy-
cotts against French products. A recent survey found that 75 percent
of U.S. households were boycotting some products—nearly half of
these because of displeasure with company policies.[28]

In June 1995, Shell UK set out to dispose of a large oil storage buoy
by sinking it in the deep ocean.[29] It had the backing of the British
government and many scientists, who had decided—after careful consideration of the environmental, safety, and economic considerations
and of the toxic materials involved—that deep-water disposal was a
better option than bringing the buoy to shore and dismantling it. Yet
other European governments opposed the disposal plan, as did environmental groups and a large segment of public opinion. The general
public seemed to feel strongly that if they were being asked to recycle
cans and bottles and not throw trash in waterways, it was simply not
appropriate to drop such a very large oil installation into the depths
of the ocean.

Shell UK gave up its disposal strategy and as of this writing was
studying alternative disposal options. Future events may prove that,
practically and scientifically, Shell UK was right in its original scheme.
Its mistake—aside from building a large object without clear, agreed
plans for its disposal or recycling—was in not taking into sufficient
account the great mass of the European public who feel they have a
say in Shell's operations.

In what may be a new trend, Shell was criticized not only by
environmental groups but by other companies. The Danish biotechnol-
ogy firm Novo Nordisk, as a signatory of the ICC Business Charter for
Sustainable Development (which called upon signatories to take some
account of their suppliers' environmental policies), issued a statement
saying it objected in principle to the dumping of industrial wastes at
sea.[30] It urged Shell to inform its various "publics," including its business partners, about the logic of its disposal plan.

John Elkington, author of *The Green Capitalists,* wrote of the Shell
case: "The controversy, which has been more about public perception
of the environmental priorities than about ecological impacts, marks
the emergence of a new era which requires business to focus on a triple
bottom line: economics, environment and social equity."

Sustainable development does go beyond environmental manage-ment into issues of equity of opportunity, so that people both now and in the future have a greater chance of meeting their needs. Calling upon business to worry about equity of opportunity and future gen-erations may seem farfetched, but in a sense business is already doing so. Several U.S. companies have been stung by reports revealing that their products are being made by children in what North Americans regard as "sweatshop" conditions. Children are certainly real-life rep-resentatives of future generations.

Child labor is an extremely complex issue, because in many devel-oping countries the choice for a child might not be between making shirts and going to school. It may be between making shirts and taking up prostitution or working in a quarry or a dangerous factory. It has been estimated that in 1993/94 between 30,000 and 50,000 children were thrown out of work in textile mills in Bangladesh because sup-pliers were worried about losing business.[31] Many of those fired went into prostitution or welding jobs. But in business, public perception remains as important as reality.

The Boston-based ethical investment firm Franklin Research and Development estimates that less than 5 percent of U.S. retailers and branded-goods companies are getting involved in human rights issues, but these include some of the biggest and best known, such as Levi, Wal-Mart, Sears Roebuck, Reebok, The Gap, Nike, and Nordstrom.[32] IKEA, the Swedish home products store, has decided the carpets it sells must be certified as made without child labor. The British-based National Provident Institution, which offers a selection of "ethical" investment programs, found in a 1995 poll of British consumers that concerns about modern slavery and abuse of workers' rights had risen above concerns for the environment and animal welfare.[33]

In fact, many companies are involved in what might be called the "social" side of sustainable development, without labelling it as such. They usually call it something like "community relations." A recent survey in Britain of companies involved in community relations work found that in the eighties this was driven by just a few enthusiastic board chairs regarded as "dotty" by their peers.[34] But "getting involved in community is no longer idiosyncratic philanthropy, not least because real commercial benefits have been seen to accrue from it," the survey concluded. It noted the case of the glass group Pilkington, which had pioneered community involvement in its region of Britain. This record was widely credited for the success of its defense against a hostile takeover in 1986–87 by a company that disdained corporate community involvement.

"Community involvement" was once restricted to big, Northern-based multinational companies. But now more developing-world companies are also practicing it. Aracruz Celulose S.A. of Brazil produces more than 1 million tons of bleached eucalyptus pulp every year from plantations on land in southern Brazil that had been deforested by farming and charcoal-making decades ago.[35] But the company also plants 27 percent of its land area in native, noncommercial tree and plant species, in order to preserve ecosystems. It supplies seedlings to local farmers and buys back the wood, but it also gives seedlings out free so farmers can meet their own wood needs without destroying the native forests. Aracruz invested $120 million to combat air and water pollution over 1992–95, and has secured international quality control certification. It has put a total of $125 million into schools, hospitals, and housing in the region, both those used by its own workers and others. It even runs ecological programs to protect the reproductive cycles of five threatened species of sea turtles.

A lot of this work is enlightened local self-interest, such as trying to keep its workers and their families healthy and well educated. Aracruz also realizes that because it is involved in forestry work and running paper mills in the developing world, it will automatically draw the attention of environmental groups. Thus it needs to be cleaner than many timber operations and paper mills operating in the remoter parts of North America. It spends a great deal of money communicating its environmental and social programs to the rest of the world. As trade and markets become more open and global, a growing number of developing-world companies will pursue similar strategies.

Coming to Terms with Eco-efficiency

In grappling with the immediate goal of eco-efficiency and the more ambitious and all-embracing goal of sustainable development, business groups have had to consider several complex issues. These include such things as internalizing environmental costs, the polluter pays principle, and greater use of economic instruments.

The concept of internalizing environmental costs has an important bearing on the relationship between financial markets and eco-efficiency. At the first BCSD meeting, in 1991, the group had difficulty knowing what advice to offer the 1992 Earth Summit, given the political, scientific, and financial uncertainties surrounding environment and development issues. What could a group of CEOs, all of whom were dedicated to free and open market systems, helpfully say?

At this point, one member argued that, as the group favored open, competitive markets, it should recommend the internalizing of environmental costs, so that markets would better reflect environmental as well as economic truths. This provided the Council with a logical way into the debate.

The concept is simple, the reality much more complex. The idea is that the price of a good or service should reflect all the costs associated with it. For example, the cost of electricity from a coal-fired power station rarely reflects the costs of the damage done by the acid rain it causes, or the health problems related to its pollution. These are real costs. It has been estimated that every ton of sulfur dioxide emitted into the atmosphere in the United States causes more than $3,000 worth of health-related damage in affected communities.[36] Thus the sulfur dioxide emissions from midwestern coal-fired power plants cost society nearly $25 billion per year. This figure is merely a rough guess, but it is clear that real money is involved and that someone must pay these costs, which have traditionally been "external" to the financial considerations of the utilities.

There appears to be an inevitable move toward more internalization of costs. In late 1994, Britain's Royal Commission on Environmental Pollution recommended that the price of gasoline should double over the coming decade. It said the cost of driving a car must increase because at the moment "it does not reflect the damage done to health and the environment."[37] The Commission even suggested that new technology be used that would allow fuel pumps to "read" a car's technical data, so that a motorist driving a highly polluting car would pay more at the pump for its fuel.

As early as 1972, OECD members agreed to the polluter pays principle (PPP), which says simply that polluters should bear the full costs of any damage caused by their production of goods and services. The principle, though ever more widely accepted, has been unevenly applied. Indeed, governments even subsidize many forms of environmental damage, such as the overuse and misuse of water, energy, pesticides, and fertilizer. In early 1994, the German government renewed until the end of the century its subsidies for coal, which had been due to expire in 1995.[38]

The BCSD has endorsed PPP and the notion of internalizing environmental costs. The Council wrote in its 1992 book *Changing Course* that "the cornerstone of sustainable development is a system of open, competitive markets in which prices are made to reflect the costs of environmental as well as other resources."[39]

The Council went on to endorse the idea of a greater use of economic instruments as a way of achieving these goals. Traditionally, governments' main tool for achieving environmental goals has been command-and-control regulations; these often tell a company precisely what technology to use and precisely what can be emitted and in what quantities. There will always be a need for such restrictions in situations where major risks and uncertainties exist. Yet environmental goals may also be achieved through economic instruments such as taxes, charges, and tradable permits. Properly applied, such instruments can help meet four needs: "to provide incentives for continuous improvements and continuous rewards, to use markets more effectively in achieving environmental objectives, to find more cost-effective ways for both government and industry to achieve these same objectives, and to move from pollution control to pollution prevention," according to *Changing Course.*

A regulation requires a company to reach a certain standard and then do no more. A tax or charge on pollution or resource use encourages a company to become ever more eco-efficient by producing a steady effect on that company's profit and loss figures.

There is a growing consensus that the use of economic instruments is increasing and that—if the instruments are well constructed and combined well with other approaches—this is a good thing.

"One example of new approaches to environmental management is the increasing use in recent years of market-based instruments such as pollution charges, or user fees and taxes on environmental goods and services," noted a 1995 U.N. Environment Programme report.[40] "The concept of using economic instruments to solve environmental problems is compelling: unless the pricing and market failures associated with environmental degradation are tackled, environmental policy will continue to work on the insufficient level of addressing the *symptoms* of environmental problems, without addressing the economic causes."

"Market based instruments are best in principle and often in practice," wrote the World Bank in 1992.[41] "Most now agree that market based instruments have been under-utilized. They are particularly promising for developing countries, which cannot afford to incur the unnecessary extra costs of less flexible instruments that have been borne by OECD countries."

Business seems to agree. "Making market forces work to protect and improve the quality of the environment—with the help of performance-based standards and the judicious use of economic instruments in a harmonious regulatory framework—is one of the greatest opportunities that the world faces in this decade," wrote the International Chamber of Commerce in 1992.[42]

Another "internalizing" activity is being carried out at both national and international levels as governments experiment with ways of making national accounts better reflect environmental reality. Standard national accounts (SNAs) follow internationally agreed rules so that they are comparable. Yet it has long been recognized that such activities as spending money on cleaning up pollution or treating people with illnesses caused by pollution increases GNP, and a growing GNP is often mistaken for "progress."

Money earned from harvesting natural resources also adds to the GNP, yet there is no accounting for the depletion of those resources, such as oil, timber, water, or topsoil. This approach should seem odd to anyone who thinks about it. It is like a person estimating how prosperous he or she is by looking only at income, not at net worth, not at assets such as a home or savings. It is perfectly possible to increase your income by selling off assets, but it is usually done only after careful consideration. Yet through such accounting devices as GNP, countries estimate how well off they are without considering how fast they are ploughing through key resources.

Individual countries such as Norway, France, and Japan have experimented with new forms of national accounting that get around some of these faults. The United Nations, which is the main standards body for SNAs, is also working on a new system of national accounting.[43] To change these accounts will require governments to seek from companies ever more information on resource use and pollution. These revelations may have an effect on how customers value some companies, and in turn on how they are valued by the financial markets.

Another idea whose time seems to be coming is that of a "tax shift." Again, the basic idea is simple: move away from taxing, and therefore discouraging, good things such as employment and the creation of capital, and move toward taxing, and discouraging, pollution and the misuse of resources. In reality it is extremely difficult to tax the misuse of resources without taxing their use in general. The political Right argues that raising taxes on such things as fossil fuels, or even on the carbon they emit, would be bad for the economy. The Left argues that it would be bad for the relatively poor, who usually spend a higher proportion of their income than the wealthy on heating their homes and fuelling their cars. Those in favor of a tax shift maintain that it is possible to devise a system that benefits the economy and the environment without overtaxing the poor.

One fact probably sums up the reason why more and more political and business leaders are willing to discuss, and even promote, the idea of a tax shift: widespread unemployment. The environment topped German opinion polls through the eighties as the main issue of concern. By late 1994 it had fallen to third; crime was second, and unemployment first. Germany taxes employment harder than most countries, but such rates are high throughout Europe. It was with the aim of decreasing unemployment that former European Union head Jacques Delors—not known as an environmental or any other type of radical—called for a shift from employment tax to resource tax.[44]

BCSD members could not bring themselves in 1992 to support the idea, partly because of its novelty and partly because of suspicion that any resource/pollution tax would be an add-on and not a shift. *Changing Course* insists on revenue neutrality: any new pollution tax must be balanced by a decrease in another tax.

Yet a 1994 BCSD report called on governments to adopt a number of national sustainable development strategies incorporating "new and flexible market based approaches," including "a tax shift away from labour and investment to value-depleting activities such as pollution and the inefficient use of environmental resources."[45]

Tax shifts have been talked about—and so far defeated—in both the United States and the European Union. But there is a widespread feeling that they are inevitable. If other CEOs change their minds as quickly as many of those who belong to the WBCSD have, then a tax shift may be a reality in much of the world by the turn of the century or soon after.

All This . . . and the Financial Markets

Imagine for a moment that the majority of environmental costs are internalized so that they are borne by companies and passed along to consumers. Imagine that governments make greater use of economic instruments to reward continuously companies that are becoming increasingly more eco-efficient, while punishing those that are not. Imagine that growing numbers of governments revise national accounting systems to reflect environmental damage and resource depletion accurately. Finally, imagine tax shifts toward the discouragement of pollution and resource overuse.

Then it is not hard to imagine that the balance sheets of companies would also change strikingly. Whole business sectors would change the ways in which they do business.

As these changes occurred, the financial markets would change the basis on which they decide whether to invest in, lend to, and insure companies. Financial markets would not have to care about "the environment"; they could assume that if a company were financially successful in a world of internalized environmental costs and taxes on pollution, then it must also be eco-efficient.

This is not going to happen quickly. In fact, it would be a mistake if such a complex set of changes were pushed along too fast. Business in general and the WBCSD in particular want to see a gradual, scheduled, predictable introduction of changes to allow business time to plan and adapt.

The various trends outlined here—internalizing environmental costs, greater use of economic instruments, new national accounts, new bases of taxation, new attention to financial markets by "the greens"—

are clearly the direction society is moving in. The more forward-looking firms are investing in eco-efficiency, and then joining groups calling for more economic instruments and the internalizing of environmental costs so that their investments will pay off sooner in financial terms. Change will, as always in major societal shifts, accelerate and decelerate and will occur faster in some places and some business sectors than in others. But businesses that do not keep up with such changes will suffer.

So, too, will the lagging players in the financial community. They will become more prone to risk and liabilities, and they will miss opportunities as they fail to see closer links between environmental quality and financial quality.

We worried at the beginning of this chapter that the workings of the financial markets encourage short-termism. But managers of pension funds are today making equity investments on behalf of people who will not collect the benefits for decades. It is quite probable that these trends will have shifted the bottom lines of many businesses considerably within a single decade. That is why the more progressive actors in the financial markets will begin to consider the implications of sustainable development now, rather than waiting for these implications to be forced on them by changes in fiscal, legal, and business realities.

"In a way, it is not even much of a stretch," wrote Richard House in *Institutional Investor*.[46] "If you believe in the advance of free markets, and you acknowledge that economic activity has environmental costs for which business is increasingly (if imperfectly) being held accountable, doesn't it seem likely that the financial markets will begin to systematically consider those costs when they value businesses? For acquisitions, this is already standard practice."

In the next chapter, we take a very general look at the roles of the financial markets in sustainable economic development in the developing world. Then in part II we go on to see how the trends discussed here are affecting various key players in the financial community. Part III offers a summary of some of the book's themes.

2   Financial Markets and the Development Process

Western [financial] firms are keenly exporting their goods and ideas to new markets. . . . They are the shock troops of capitalism, if not of democracy. Their techniques and their intermediation are binding the world and its markets together as never before. The goal is a single market for risk.

Andrew Freeman, *The Economist,*
April 15, 1995

The so-called emerging markets are mainly emerging in the developing world, where population growth is fastest and where soil, water, forest, and other ecosystems are most under threat. (Given that so much has been written about the "mature" financial markets, and given that we emphasize them in the rest of our book, we focus here on risks and opportunities in financing development in the developing world.)

Creating a harmony between the ecological and efficiency imperatives of the emerging-market economies will require that the processes of capital formation and allocation favor rather than inhibit eco-efficiency. This will in turn require the spread of global standards, the integration of sustainable development factors into financial-sector reform programs, financial innovation, and widespread capacity-building efforts.

Encouraging policymakers and market participants toward eco-efficiency will require substantial support from the bilateral and multilateral development banks and agencies, not so much because of the funding they can contribute as for the influence they can yield in accelerating a process of change that has only just begun.

There is confusion over the term "emerging markets." Most financial newspapers and journals that cover them specify about two dozen

Chapter 2 Summary

In nations with threatened ecosystems and rapidly growing populations, emerging financial markets must encourage eco-efficiency to conserve resources and limit pollution. Given the expense that today's industrial countries have had to bear for cleanups, developing economies cannot afford to pollute now and clean up later.

Developing regions are already liberalizing trade and foreign investment regimes while pursuing privatization schemes and opening new financial markets. They are expected to grow twice as fast as the industrial world in the coming decade, but only if they can maintain financial discipline.

Yet questions remain over whether the new surge of portfolio investment is short-term. Will it encourage wise use of natural resources? Will it increase pollution or provide the means of controlling it?

Emerging-market companies are releasing more environmental information as they try to raise capital in the Euromarkets and in the United States. But shortages of capital, information, and expertise are hampering the diffusion of cleaner production in the developing world. Companies will not be moved to overcome these obstacles without tough governmental antipollution regimes.

Innovative partnerships among companies, governments, and multilateral agencies are providing capital in new ways: public-private financing partnerships, financial-sector reform programs, and privatization schemes with technical help. Emerging-economy governments are beginning to push through their own programs of investment guarantees, energy service programs, convertible grants, and support for venture capital programs. But a great deal more needs to be done.

countries with new or recently significant equity markets, mainly in the developing world. The *Economist*, for example, lists in its weekly emerging-market section the 10 better-off Asian nations; Argentina, Brazil, Chile, Mexico, and Venezuela in Latin America; and the Czech Republic, Hungary, Poland, and Russia among the formerly socialist countries. But it also includes Greece, Israel, Portugal, South Africa, and Turkey.

The United Nations and some other multilateral agencies, apparently trying not to hurt any nation's feelings, tend to define all markets not in the highly industrial nations of Australasia, North America, and Western Europe as "emerging." Thus according to the International Monetary Fund (IMF), there are 153 emerging markets (really, national economies), which produce 45.6 percent of world output.[1] By comparison, the industrial economies number 23 and account for the other 54.4 percent of world output. "Emerging economies" in this system means the 130 developing countries of Asia-Pacific, the Western Hemisphere, the Middle East, and Africa, which together produce about one third of world output, as well as the 23 formerly centrally planned economies of Central and Eastern Europe, the former Soviet Union, and Mongolia. The latter together produce just over one tenth of world output and are sometimes known as the "transition economies."

We shall use "emerging markets" in the more journalistic sense and use "developing world" to refer to the nations that the IMF also categorizes as emerging. (See map on page 32.)

The private sector is now almost universally recognized as the engine of economic growth and development. As a result, developing-country governments are encouraging liberalization, privatization, and fiscal reform and are emphasizing a more intensive participation in the world economic system. In 1995, the World Bank predicted that during the next decade, real economic growth rates in the Northern economies would be 3 percent a year, while developing economies would grow by 6 percent.[2] The forecast depended on developing-world governments exercising considerable economic discipline while continuing to liberalize their economies. The report commented: "The premium on sound economic policies has risen. In a more integrated global economy, the rewards of such policies are larger, but so are the penalties for policy errors."

The shift to greater reliance on market forces in the developing world is taking place at a dramatic pace. For example:

• 63 developing economies have liberalized their trade policy regimes since the Uruguay Round of the General Agreement on Tariffs and Trade (GATT) talks began in 1985,

• more than 30 liberalized their foreign direct investment regimes in 1991 alone,

• more than 60 currently have active privatization programs, and

• more than 50 have established capital markets in the nineties.[3]

Liberalization, privatization, and fiscal reform are all expressions of the fundamental shift in policy orientation in developing countries that

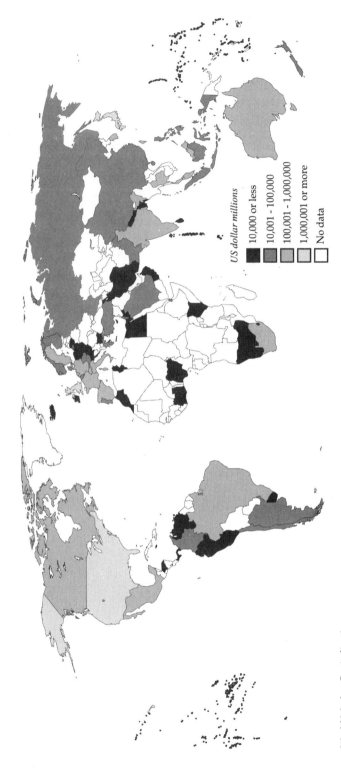

US dollar millions

- ■ 10,000 or less
- ▨ 10,001 - 100,000
- ▦ 100,001 - 1,000,000
- ▢ 1,000,001 or more
- □ No data

World Market Capitalization
Source: International Finance Corporation

is driving the economic growth rates just mentioned. Naturally, this shift is throwing up new business opportunities for local and foreign entrepreneurs, and these bring new openings for local and foreign investors.

Many such opportunities are being created by the privatization of direct state involvement in the economy. Private companies are being invited to own and operate state-owned enterprises, many of which offer tremendous commercial potential if managed with modern business know-how. For the period 1989–93, privatization transactions in developing economies added up to $56 billion, about 25 percent of this being foreign capital.[4] The privatization process is most dramatic in Eastern and Central Europe. But there are also widespread privatization programs in Latin America, more recent ones in Africa and South Asia, and some in China as well.

Private Capital Flows

Corporate and institutional investors are recognizing the rapid growth rates and enormous changes in policy taking place in developing economies. For the developing world to achieve the growth rates predicted by the World Bank, huge amounts of capital will be needed. Although most of this will come from domestic savings, McKinsey estimates that the developing economies as a whole will need to import $2 trillion ($2,000 billion) over the coming decade.[5]

These and other considerations, such as the strategic restructuring of industries away from high-cost economies to lower-cost developing ones, have dramatically increased the number of companies investing across national borders. There are now approximately 40,000 multinational corporations, most of which are small and medium-sized.[6] Although about 90 percent of them originate in the North, half of their foreign affiliates are based in developing economies.

As a group, developing economies have been enjoying patterns of foreign direct and portfolio investment in the nineties more favorable than in the three decades since the decolonization process began. As noted in chapter 1, in 1994 the flow of private capital into the developing countries was as high as $170 billion, according to the World Bank.[7]

Initially, private investment flows were driven by foreign direct investment (FDI)—multinational companies investing in joint ventures and projects and establishing subsidiaries in the developing world. More recently, there has been phenomenal growth in foreign portfolio investment in developing economies, including investment in securities such as equities and bonds by foreign individuals and institutions. These may be more volatile than FDI.

Capitalization of developing stock markets has leapt tenfold since 1985 to $1.9 trillion at the end of 1994, compared with $13.2 trillion for the industrial economies.[8] There has also been strong growth in foreign portfolio investment: $200 billion of developing-market equities were held by foreigners at the end of 1993, compared with just $2.1 billion in 1986, according to Baring Securities.[9] U.S. investors account for about two thirds of the current total. These flows, which averaged less than $6 billion annually in the period 1982–88, were estimated at $21 billion in 1992 and just above $62 billion in 1993. The World Institute for Development Economics Research expects annual new portfolio investment in developing economies will grow to $100 billion by the end of this decade.[10] International bank lending has also been recovering from the debt crisis of the eighties.

So far, equity flows to developing stock markets have been restricted to a handful of countries—the emerging markets. Nevertheless, smaller markets such as Peru and Zimbabwe are also beginning to attract volumes of capital that, although small by international standards, are significant in local terms.

The emerging capital markets have become a key area of interest for international investors everywhere, and financial institutions are developing products and expertise in emerging economies. Yet the fashion over the past few years of diversifying investments into emerging markets is nothing new. According to Baring Securities, the average portfolio of a British institutional investor in 1913 had 54 percent invested in emerging-market securities (Latin America, 20.1 percent; Asia and Africa, mainly South Africa, 22.5 percent), and only 2.4 percent in Western Europe.[11]

The Institute for International Finance thinks we are witnessing the beginning of a large portfolio shift that could last 10–15 years.[12] The World Bank report referred to earlier noted that "it may take some time for confidence in emerging markets to be re-established following the Mexican crisis, but in the medium term, private capital flows to developing countries are expected to resume growth, albeit at a slower pace."[13] Emerging-market countries and companies are themselves directly accessing international financial markets and raising substantial amounts of capital through, for example, bond issues in the Euromarkets.

International development agencies have been involved in helping to create the regulatory framework to facilitate the flows. In particular, they have encouraged the development of the private sector and the freeing of controls on capital through their structural adjustment programs, and they have advised on and funded financial-sector reform, including the development of stock exchanges.

One of the drawbacks to all this good news is that foreign portfolio investment in the emerging market economies is volatile. Whereas equity investors focusing on the United States may switch companies, emerging-market investors are more likely to switch countries instead. This happened at the end of 1994, when investors suddenly lost faith in Mexico when the peso was devalued and pulled out in such numbers that the United States had to arrange a financial rescue package. Mexico's troubles sent irrational ripples of unease throughout the equity markets of Latin America. A much touted country can also attract too much capital too quickly, driving up inflation and causing the currency to become overvalued. China and Vietnam are textbook examples of this type of overheating. And foreign portfolio investment can squeeze local small and medium-scale enterprises when governments feel compelled to jack up the interest rates on bonds in order to keep foreign capital flowing in.

Foreign Investment and Sustainable Development

Looking at the recent leaps in foreign investment in the developing world, it is easy to forget that these countries are home to more than 1 billion people living on an annual per capita income of $350 or less. Many of these poor are in big countries enjoying investment attention, such as China, India, South Africa, and Brazil. Many are in countries receiving virtually no investments, such as large parts of sub-Saharan

Africa north of South Africa. In the last quarter of 1993, global emerging-market funds held just 0.3 percent of their assets in African investments, according to a survey by Micropal.[14] So the poorest countries are receiving virtually no investments to make up for the fall in international aid documented in chapter 1.

Poverty remains the number one obstacle to sustainable development. In a 1993 report on Latin America, the World Bank noted that the region has the most unequal income distribution in the world, with the poorest 20 percent of the population receiving about 4 percent of the income.[15] It warned governments that "failures to act aggressively on poverty will likely encourage distributive conflicts, prompting discontent and perhaps even a return to populism . . . and chaos." Thus it is crucial for developing-country governments to establish systems that create equity of opportunity so that as many people as possible share in the increasing wealth.

With more than 90 percent of the world's population growth in the nineties projected to take place in developing economies, the urgency of the situation can only increase. The alarming deterioration of much of the natural resource base of these countries is set to go on. Pollution levels are already a major threat to public health and are making some areas in Poland, Taiwan, Thailand, Mexico, and other countries virtually uninhabitable.

The unmet basic needs of the majority of the people in the developing economies are staggering:

- 1.3 billion people lack access to clean water,
- 2 billion people do not have safe sanitation,
- some 800 million people go to bed hungry every night, and
- there is one doctor for every 7,000 people, compared with one for every 400 people in industrial countries.[16]

Such figures show why sustainable development, though a goal for both developing and industrial nations, has such an immediacy in the poorer countries. Given present needs and reasonable aspirations, plus the rapidly increasing needs of rapidly increasing populations, more capital is obviously a necessary condition for sustainable development. But it is hardly a sufficient condition. In fact, the liberalization of these economies could well encourage the unsustainable exploitation of their natural resources by local and international companies.

The interplay between portfolio investment and sustainable development raises a number of key questions:

• Is foreign portfolio investment driven by the short-term ability to exploit undervalued assets (such as natural resources) in an unsustainable way, and is it accelerating that process? Or is it more driven by the prospects for long-term growth?

• Is foreign investment increasing pollution, by encouraging the expansion of polluting industries in areas where regulation is weak? Or does it provide the much needed capital to make the investments necessary to reduce environmental impacts?

• Is foreign investment increasing social divisions and mainly benefiting the rich? Or is it helping development more broadly, including the creation of quality jobs and the development of a middle class?

• Is foreign portfolio investment making domestic capital and investment in developing economies more short-term in its focus by encouraging financial speculation that diverts funds from, say, small and medium-sized enterprises? Or is it contributing to long-term financial development?

We would like to answer these questions, but cannot. The phenomenon of foreign investment in such amounts is too new, and the long-term results cannot be known. Research into effects on the environment and on social organization is only just beginning.

Across much of the developing world, environmental protection increasingly depends on private-sector participation and leadership (for example, in such areas as water infrastructure and clean power generation). Meeting these challenges will require innovative financing structures (such as leasing, BOT [build-operate-transfer] deals, guarantees, and venture capital) to reduce risks and facilitate capital formation.

Most developing market economies are rich in natural resources. But in many sectors of these economies, resources are not harvested sustainably; rather, they are mined by local and international companies for immediate returns. The shrimp farming industry in Thailand is a graphic example of expansion of an industry being limited due to unsustainable harvesting.[17] While scarce natural capital is inadequately priced by the market in industrial economies, as discussed in chapter 1, the situation is even worse in the developing world.

Global Integration and Trends

The global financial market is rapidly becoming more integrated, and thus better at allocating capital to its most productive uses. A more efficient global financial market should be better able to match savings in the North with the hugely profitable investment opportunities in emerging economies. As the markets become more integrated, the prices of financial instruments with identical risks should converge across markets.

Yet because of the novelty of this integration, its speed is often exaggerated. Martin Feldstein, president of the National Bureau of Economic Research in the United States, argues that "capital may be free to move internationally, but its owners and managers prefer to keep almost all of each nation's savings at home. Future policy in Mexico and elsewhere must take that key fact as its starting point."[18] He adds that much of the capital that does move internationally "is pursuing temporary gains and shifts quickly as conditions change. The patient money that will support sustained cross-border capital flows is surprisingly scarce." If capital still balks at crossing borders in seeking its long-term highest rate of return, this will hamper the development of emerging markets for some time to come.

However, both the global integration of markets and deregulation in the industrial world are having the odd effect of increasing pressure for an international set of financial market regulations that will affect emerging markets.[19] National regulators once resisted international standards. But they seem to be coming to terms with the fact that the present interdependence means the collapse of a financial services company in one country could bring down others elsewhere.

Andrew Large, chairman of the U.K. Securities and Investment Board, says that he sees a "significant change in mindset" among his fellow regulators.[20] "It is coming home to people that the international and domestic agendas are becoming very much the same. . . . No one market supervisor has the full picture [about] groups that are operating globally." After a meeting in Paris of the International Organisation of Securities Commissions in mid-1995, a grouping of insurance, bank, and securities regulators known as the Tripartite Group issued a report wondering if traditional approaches to financial regulation were "still appropriate."[21] It said: "Intensive cooperation between supervisors is essential and supervisors should have the right to exchange prudential information."

International coordination of regulations will mean that emerging markets face tougher standards to convince investors that their financial houses are in order. For example, Paraguay, which returned to civilian rule as recently as 1993, developed during its decades of dictatorship a corrupt and lax banking system. Yet in 1995, when $4.5 million went missing from the central bank, the government took the unprecedented step of firing the entire bank directorate.[22] Interim central bank president Dionisio Coronel promised to push through a new banking law to "incorporate the Basle norms for classifying portfolios and to establish the necessity of external audits." All over the developing world, governments are trying to improve investor confidence by tightening up regulations in the banking and securities sectors, as well as improving legal systems to instill confidence in contractual agreements.

Disclosure of environmental information is looming as a vital issue for financial regulators and institutional investors in the industrial world. But corporations in developing economies have generally had to disclose little financial and even less environmental information publicly, as they have typically raised capital through private placements and borrowings. Greater financial disclosure by emerging-economy corporations is being fostered by their efforts to raise capital in the Euromarkets and in the United States through American Depositary Receipts.[23]

As the emerging stock markets mature and come under tighter regulatory control, companies seeking a listing will have to disclose greater amounts of and more detailed financial information. There is also an opportunity to ensure that environmental disclosure standards are accepted by the emerging markets both to spur eco-efficiency among local corporations and to help secure the level regulatory playing field desired by companies based in the North. It will be interesting to see if the World Trade Organization can, as it tries to "green the GATT," help to harmonize environmental reporting requirements among countries.

Investors and lenders in the developing world are becoming more aware of environmental issues, as evidenced by a turnout of 150 financial professionals at a seminar on finance and the environment organized in Manila in February 1994.[24] They are being influenced by tightening domestic environmental regulations, increasing consumer pressure arising from a growing middle class, and a dawning recognition that poor environmental performance can affect the ability of local companies to compete in the lucrative markets of the industrial world. Like their counterparts in the North, however, they are predominantly concerned with the downside of the environmental challenge, hoping to avoid liability for past and future environmental damage.

Very few emerging-market financial institutions yet see much upside investment potential in the environment, and fewer still are familiar with the concept and benefits of eco-efficiency. Typically, they are handicapped by an acute shortage of environmental risk management expertise and a lack of knowledge about eco-efficient technology. Only a handful of emerging-market countries can draw on a well-developed pool of environmental auditors, consultants, researchers, or pressure groups that financial institutions can work with to better understand and deal with environmental issues.

Better information is a key to mobilizing the financial markets in favor of eco-efficiency in the emerging markets. Although information flows are improving, too many of the information systems established so far are either unknown to emerging-market financiers or are inaccessible because the information is provided in ways that do not speak to their culture and requirements as financial professionals. This may change as computing power becomes less expensive and as communications links become cheaper, more sophisticated, and more secure.

Banks have been rapidly computerizing both their back-office managing of money and their communications with customers. Automated teller machines outside of or far from branches and telephone banking not only permit 24-hour banking, they allow banks to deal more efficiently with the individual needs and concerns of customers. In other words, computers help banks move from transaction to "relationship" banking. This may help banks in the developing world expand into remote areas or even into urban slums without setting up an expensive branch system. We offer examples in chapter 5 of banks in Africa using high-tech solutions to gain customers among the urban poor.

Security companies and banks in the North are increasingly using "value at risk" computer programs, or models, to track variables such as currency and interest rate fluctuations and provide early warning of developing risks.[25] Such models also make it easier to manage derivatives (options, futures, and so on). As they become cheaper and more easily available, they will also help financial communities in the developing world improve rapidly their management of risks.

Financing Eco-efficiency in the Developing World

Difficulties in access to finance are hampering the diffusion of cleaner production technologies. Small and medium-sized enterprises, in particular, have a hard time making cleaner production investments for a variety of reasons, ranging from the cost of capital to the absence of appropriate funding instruments. Furthermore, eco-efficiency is less able to pay for itself in countries with few and lax environmental regulations, underpriced or free environmental resources, and no green consumer movement.

Traditionally, environmental technology investments have, at best, been viewed as simply a cost of complying with environmental regulations. As a result, those that have been made have typically been the "end-of-pipe" type. The idea of the environment being a source of competitive advantage is, therefore, a relatively new one, requiring business executives and financiers to develop new perspectives, concepts, and operational tools. It also requires governments to set up a regulatory system that does not make large-scale pollution a viable business option. This is beginning to happen. In India, for instance, the new environmental policy announced in 1993 as part of the country's economic liberalization program places the emphasis of government tax incentives and regulations on cleaner production by industry.[26]

High economic growth rates provide businesses with the opportunity to improve the eco-efficiency of their operations and also mean faster turnover of industrial plant. Between 1994 and 2010, up to 85 percent of Asia's installed industrial base and perhaps 70 percent of its energy-producing capacity will be new, the World Bank estimates.[27] Investments in plant modernization generally lead to lower pollution intensities, since new processes and plants typically use fewer inputs, are more efficient, and rely on more materials recycling than older technologies. Clean technologies installed in new plants often pay for themselves in terms of both lower input costs and improved competitiveness in light of new product specifications. End-of-pipe pollution control equipment rarely pays for itself, however. Developing countries have strategic opportunities to adopt cleaner production as part of their efforts to industrialize and increase international competitiveness.

The developing world must seize this opportunity, as it simply cannot afford the loss of resources and the pollution damage caused by traditional patterns of industrial development. In industrial nations, the costs of waste management are a heavy burden on economies. By reducing this hardship through cleaner production, developing countries can boost their international competitiveness while maintaining environmental quality. Whether they can "leapfrog" the North in this way depends greatly on the types of technologies they choose to adopt (and adapt), as well as the availability of sufficient amounts of appropriate financing.

If developing nations opt for investment in more resource-efficient equipment, combined with cleaner technologies to prevent pollution rather than end-of-pipe devices to control it, they could reduce by 25–50 percent their costs of complying with environmental standards, according to the U.N. Industrial Development Organization.[28] Clearly, developing countries need information that will help them take advantage of these potential cost reductions.

At the micro level, however, companies with weak balance sheets and limited access to external finance are usually reluctant to replace and write-down existing equipment in favor of more modern technologies. Even where the benefits are manifest, the upfront capital costs can be prohibitive, especially for smaller companies, which are typically in a weak position to seek long-term financing for capital expenditures.

According to research by the Organisation for Economic Co-operation and Development, even when eco-efficient technologies offer lower operating costs, many companies lack sufficient cash flow to invest in them.[29] This problem appears to be most acute in the high-debt countries of Latin America and central and eastern Europe, and in countries with limited reserves of foreign exchange. As a result, some governments seem reluctant to strengthen or enforce environmental regulations fully because they fear that companies would find it financially impossible to comply with them.

International Development Agencies

Funds from the international development agencies—the bilateral and multilateral development banks, and the multilateral and bilateral aid providers—represent a relatively small proportion of the total capital going into the developing economies, except for the poorest.

These "aid agencies" can, nevertheless, have an impact on policies and investment decisions in the developing world disproportionate to the amount of funding they provide. This is because more and more aid (out of a steadily shrinking total supply) is provided in exchange for policy reform. Aid flows signal confidence in a country's prospects; aid unlocks private capital sometimes in a ratio of up to 6:1 for aid-supported projects; and aid can be used to pioneer new approaches to financing that can be emulated by non-aid resources.[30] Aid can mobilize the financial markets to promote eco-efficiency in the developing world in three main ways: partnerships, financial-sector reform, and privatization.

Public-Private Financing Partnerships

The higher the perceived risks of investing in emerging economies, the shorter are the investors' and lenders' time horizons and the higher must be their expected rates of return. As a result, many eco-efficient investments can appear unattractive to private investors. Aid can be used to reduce risks, to lengthen maturities, and to reduce the price of capital.

In many cases, investors are deterred from putting funds into infrastructure in developing markets due to perceptions of excessively high noncommercial risks, especially in the poorer countries. Aid funds can be matched for foreign direct investment projects through joint ventures that build and operate facilities, including environment and energy infrastructure; they can also be used for guarantees against sovereign risks, matched with private capital for venture capital investment in technology start-ups, and so on.

A number of innovative partnerships initiated over the past few years point the way forward.[31] The Global Environment Emerging Markets Fund (GEEMF) was the first of its kind to offer public guarantee of capital for environmental risk investments in developing economies. The Washington-based Global Environment Fund Management Corporation raised $75 million from institutional investors in 1994 on the back of $50 million of investment guarantees underwritten by the Overseas Private Investment Corporation (OPIC), a U.S. government agency. The GEEMF planned to invest in 140 developing economies in companies involved in developing environmental infrastructure and clean energy projects, especially in the areas of water and wastewater treatment, natural gas and renewable energy, and industrial process efficiency. The fund wants to identify bottlenecks to development that are both environmental and economic in nature, as with cleaner energy and clean water. It also looks at a wide range of environmental industries, including air pollution prevention, waste minimization, industrial process and energy efficiency, eco-tourism, and sustainable use of natural resources.

The Nordic Environmental Finance Corporation (NEFCO) was established by the five Nordic countries to provide risk capital for long-term cooperation between Nordic and East European enterprises on environmental technology. The company has a capital base of $50 million and can participate in up to 35 percent of the equity of a joint venture, as long as commercial partners participate on equal terms. NEFCO can also provide funding for feasibility studies and mobilize additional debt for projects.

The North American Environmental Fund (NAEF) is a $100-million fund managed by California-based Ventana Environmental Corporation, together with Nafin, Mexico's largest development bank. It is a limited partnership created in 1993 to invest in environmental technology joint ventures between Mexican and U.S. companies. The Japanese Overseas Economic Cooperation Fund has invested $25 million. The principal focus of NAEF is on financing environmental infrastructure on the BOT approach and its associated technology transfer. Ventana anticipated that NAEF would attract $300 million in co-invested private equity capital and possibly as much as $1 billion of project financing.

Several other initiatives are in the advanced stage of development. The Asia Sustainable Growth Fund is being developed by the Asian Development Bank (ADB). Anticipated to raise $150 million, the fund plans to invest in the emerging economies of the Pacific Rim. The objective is to generate financially attractive returns and to provide a source of long-term capital for eco-efficient companies in the region. The fund would be handled by a private-sector manager and is expected to attract both official and private capital. The ADB is also planning to sponsor a support mechanism called the Asia Sustainable Project Development Facility to help prepare and identify suitable investment projects for the fund and for other investors.

The Calvert Emerging Europe Fund for Sustainable Development is being sponsored by the founders of the $4-billion socially invested family of funds. Backed by OPIC, this fund intends to raise $60 million for venture capital investments in high-growth businesses in Central and Eastern Europe that contribute to sustainable development.

The ENDA Southern Africa Sustainable Investments Fund is sponsored by an economic development trust in Zimbabwe. It intends to invest up to $30 million in South African and Zimbabwean enterprises that add value to natural resources or that use eco-efficient technologies. Capital is to be raised from development banks and private institutions; donors are expected to subsidize the costs of setting up a professionally managed investment company to operate the first and successor funds.

All these comprise a small but growing number of public-private financial mechanisms partly supported by aid agencies that are aimed at the development and diffusion of cleaner production technologies.

These initiatives represent more than additional capital; they are innovative models in themselves. They also provide an opportunity to demonstrate that clean technology investments increase the competitiveness of investee companies. Nevertheless, the funds currently being mobilized for clean technology investments in the developing economies come nowhere close to meeting the potential demand for such investments.

Financial-Sector Reform Programs

The World Bank, the International Monetary Fund, and the regional development banks are fostering financial-sector reform in developing economies through policy dialogue, loans, and technical assistance. Unfortunately, little effort has been made to date to incorporate eco-efficiency or sustainable development factors into these programs. There is also no evidence to suggest that either borrowers or lenders understand the merits of doing so, although the European Bank for Reconstruction and Development and the International Finance Corporation (IFC) have small programs of technical assistance for training bank managers in transition economies and the developing world about environmental risk management.

The private-sector financing arms of the development banks, most prominently the IFC, could do much to accelerate the shift to eco-efficiency in developing economies. Investment officers are slowly becoming more culturally and technically attuned to eco-efficiency. In the past, most bank officials saw the environment as a side issue that could be adequately dealt with through liability-oriented, environmental impact assessments of projects.

Privatization

The development banks, led by the World Bank, are supporting privatization through policy and project lending as well as technical assistance. Many candidates for privatization have been burdened with contaminated sites that someone must clean up. And many others may be the source of continuing pollution flows, or may be drawing down stocks of natural resources at an alarming rate. Privatization may therefore recapitalize and revive polluting firms that would otherwise go out of business.

Of course, privatization is usually meant to produce positive effects, such as increased efficiency in the use of natural resources and more rapid adoption of cleaner technologies. At present, the World Bank advises governments to assume responsibility for most or all damages or hazards resulting from past practices, thus providing the new owner with a "clean slate."[32] Many private investors insist on special concessions such as reductions in price and indemnifications; others are willing to undertake cleanup if reimbursed from purchase funds. While governments, donors, and investors work through the legal and financial complexities of environmental liabilities associated with privatization candidates, opportunities for structuring eco-efficiency factors into the process can be missed.

Eco-efficiency can be incorporated into the structuring, negotiating, and financing of privatization programs and tenders. Rather than awarding tenders to the highest bidder or to the bid with the lowest cost of service provision, governments could weight decisions with eco-efficiency investments and improvements in mind. This might also help overcome political obstacles where foreign ownership is an issue. Turning this concept into practice will require significant technical assistance from donors. Leverage over the policymakers in recipient governments can be enhanced or backed up through lending operations.

Innovative Financial Strategies for Cleaner Energy

Although governments have a key role to play in shaping a business environment that encourages eco-efficiency, financial innovation by market participants is also required. This is true in both the industrial and the developing world, but particularly in the latter. It is true in all sectors, but the struggle for cleaner, more efficient energy systems offers some striking examples.

As developing economies liberalize their energy markets and attain macroeconomic stability, they are attracting significant amounts of capital to large energy projects. In the meantime, a financing "gap" is developing for smaller, cleaner investments. This has a variety of causes, including high transaction costs, the need of major investors to move significant volumes of capital quickly, the difficulties associated with measuring the creditworthiness of smaller projects, and institutional investors' typical lack of technological and energy market sophistication. Thus many worthwhile clean energy and energy efficiency investments face huge funding obstacles.

Energy provision can be made both cleaner and more efficient, often with considerable cost savings, by improving generation, transmission, and distribution systems. This includes introducing better managerial, operational, and maintenance practices; increasing the use of renewable energy technologies and less-polluting fuels; bringing in new equipment; and creating or manufacturing designs that use less energy.

In developing economies with low operational efficiencies in their energy sectors, technologies for plant rehabilitation, life extension, system interconnection, and improvements in transmission and distribution systems often offer higher returns to investment than do new plants. In China, for instance, there are about 400,000 small industrial boilers consuming about 300 million tons of coal per year.[33] Their efficiency is about 30 percent less than similar operations in more industrialized countries. With the right efficiency improvements, some 90 million tons of coal per year could be saved.

Stand-alone renewable energy sources, such as wind turbines and photovoltaics (PVs), are becoming more cost-competitive with diesel generators and grid extension in many parts of the developing world. These technologies are providing high-quality energy services where there are large rural populations, such as in India and China. The government of India has decided to install about 25,000 PV rural telephone systems as part of the first phase of its plan to provide telecommunications facilities in villages.[34] Where biomass residues are available, conversion technologies can also offer promising returns, with paybacks of less than three years. And small hydroelectric schemes are fast becoming a major opportunity for private-sector participation in many developing energy markets.

The clean energy and energy efficiency investments described here typically range from $500,000 to $10 million.[35] This means they are unable to tap the international financial markets or most other major sources of capital such as that available from the IFC, the arm of the

World Bank that is the largest source of direct private-sector financing in the developing world. Except in sub-Saharan Africa, the IFC does not usually consider projects smaller than $20 million.

Developing-market governments can do a great deal to attract private capital to clean energy and energy-efficiency investments. Tax regimes must reward technology upgrading and capital investment, and political and commercial risks must be minimized. But financial innovation is required to accelerate the shift toward a sustainable future. A few examples of this that are already being put into practice are investment guarantees, energy service companies, convertible grants, venture capital, sublicensing, leasing, and carbon offsets.

With investment guarantees, public agencies can guarantee the capital, but not the returns, invested in funds that then invest in clean energy projects. This can greatly lever public resources to attract private capital. As noted earlier, the guarantee by the U.S. government agency OPIC of $50 million worth of notes issued by the Global Environment Emerging Markets Fund enabled its sponsors to raise more than $70 million in less than three months from small institutional investors and medium-sized fiduciary trusts.[36]

Energy service companies (ESCos) are paid from the savings generated from demand-side management programs. Generally, ESCos are responsible for financing the cost of retrofitting and other energy efficiency measures. Efforts have recently been made to establish such companies in the developing world, particularly in India.[37]

One of the main obstacles to enterprise-driven technology transfers is the pre-investment costs associated with feasibility studies. Public agencies such as bilateral donors can make grants to cover the costs associated with establishing collaborative arrangements, which if successful can be converted into an equity or royalty stake. The resulting financial returns can then be redeployed as grants for successive projects. The Rockefeller Foundation has an ambitious program of this kind aimed at stimulating private-sector investment in renewable energy and energy efficiency enterprises across the developing world.

As noted, many cleaner energy and efficiency investments are too small to be attractive to large institutions. Venture capital companies can serve as effective technology intermediaries and conduits for mobilizing and channelling institutional capital. Venture capitalists can help create markets for products by providing a range of value-adding services to smaller companies. These funds can also serve as a window on emerging markets and technologies for strategic or corporate investors. The IFC is considering a $200-million renewable energy/energy efficiency fund, investing mainly in unlisted securities, to be privately underwritten and managed by private-sector institutions with IFC cosponsorship and participation.[38]

Few small and medium-sized enterprises in developing economies can afford clean energy and energy-efficient technologies. And many suppliers are keen to transfer their technology to more than one buyer. A single intermediary can be established to purchase technologies and then sublicense them at cost to small and medium-sized companies. Various nonprofit agencies such as Appropriate Technology International and the Intermediate Technology Development Group do this with internally developed or adapted technologies.

The total life-cycle costs of energy-efficient equipment are generally lower than those of inefficient equipment. The initial costs of efficient equipment to users, however, are usually higher. This is an important determinant where capital is scarce and expensive. Leasing is a rapidly growing, off-balance-sheet industrial financing mechanism in Asia and Latin America and could be adapted to meet the needs of clean energy and energy efficiency investments.

The Framework Convention on Climate Change envisages private and public-sector investments by organizations outside their own countries that will reduce greenhouse gas emissions in order to offset atmospheric carbon emissions in the home country. This activity comes under the convention's provisions for "joint implementation" (JI).[39] As greenhouse gas emission standards and related taxes in industrial countries rise, an increasingly large pool of capital might become available toward the end of the nineties for clean energy and energy efficiency investments in the developing economies. The Dutch and Norwegian governments have been especially active in studying options for JI, as have energy companies such as AES and TransAlta Utilities.[40]

The $1.5-billion Global Environment Facility is examining ways to spur the growth of a carbon offsets market and to accelerate foreign investment in sectors offering the opportunity for low-cost greenhouse gas mitigation, including ways in which it can alleviate the risks associated with high-risk investments.

With this range of innovative financial strategies to call on—from convertible grants to venture capital, leasing, and so on—for the establishment of a cleaner energy path than the industrial world followed, the prospects for financial markets to get involved in the development process are steadily improving.

II The Players

In this second part of the book, we look at the relationships between financial markets and eco-efficiency, examining issues that affect the roles of the different "players" in the markets: those who "lead" businesses (owners, boards, and directors); investors and analysts; bankers; insurers; accountants; and raters. It is only by looking at the roles and concerns of those in the financial community who work with and in the markets that we can stay in the domain of reality and avoid the realms of pure theory or wishful thinking.

It is helpful to keep in mind that for all parts of the financial community there are essentially two different but overlapping sets of links between the markets and sustainable development. There are issues of accounting, valuation, and liability—accounting for environmental costs and for eco-efficiency benefits. And there are the business and opportunity issues—investing in such things as eco-efficiency, sustainable forestry, renewable energy, and biodiversity prospecting.

Since we are taking a global view—and since we 120 members of the World Business Council for Sustainable Development represent a global organization but come from many different countries—we find it hard to offer specific recommendations that make sense in all markets in all cultures in all countries. Thus in part II we are mainly reporting on how certain market players are avoiding risk and taking advantage of opportunities in response to sustainability issues. And at the end of each chapter, we suggest some ways forward.

3   The Company Leaders

Those of us who have been given the privilege of developing resources, building and operating factories and plants, distributing our goods and services to the market, and advising our customers on what they should and should not buy, those of us should primarily accept responsibility for explaining the environmental impacts of our enterprises. The buck obviously stops with us.

Rodney Chase, Managing Director
British Petroleum, September 1994

An obvious place to start looking at the players affected by today's changing financial climate is by considering those who own, run, and guide the strategies of enterprises, as they are the main link between the financial markets and the environmental impacts of business. But they are a difficult starting point, as they are such a heterogeneous group. Also, businesses are organized differently in different cultures, and we shall not in a short space be able to reflect that variety adequately. Finally, the concerns of those in multinationals, in industrial-world companies, in developing-world companies, and in small and medium-sized companies are all going to be very different. (As chapter 4 is on investors, we shall leave until then a discussion of the roles of investors as owners.)

We talk in this chapter more about company leaders in general rather than focusing only on their relationship to the financial markets. This is in keeping with our view that most changes in the ways in which the financial markets relate to eco-efficiency will come from outside those markets—from society and its governments, for example—rather than from inside. Much of what we describe here concerns changes within companies that will affect their valuation by the financial markets.

Chapter 3 Summary

To take advantage of current trends, leaders of businesses must develop eco-efficiency strategies and forge strong relationships with key stake-holders.

Both efforts require long-term, strategic planning. Some company directors tend to blame financial markets for forcing them to think short term. But some in the financial community argue that the blame for short-termism lies mainly with business.

Eco-efficiency is becoming equated with good business practices for many reasons—not least being the fact that "green consumers" are switching from brand loyalty to company loyalty. Newly available data show a correlation between corporate cleanliness and financial achievement. There is even evidence that companies benefit in performance terms by getting involved in charities.

An eco-efficiency strategy, having been devised, must be communicated. Many companies still hesitate to be frank with stakeholders, so their messages are ineffective. It is certainly no longer enough to say, "We are spending a lot on the environment."

Increasing the circle of corporate stakeholders to include neighbors, citizen groups, all levels of government, and suppliers can make a company more effective, as well as less likely to be caught off guard by new developments. The goal is to focus on all the relationships that improve a company's competitiveness.

The market is a tougher master than a government, which can be lobbied and influenced. More and more, the market is becoming the ultimate arbiter of success, and more and more the market itself is demanding eco-efficiency.

Leadership for the Long Term

A move toward eco-efficiency by a business will require a strategy designed to operate over several years. It will also require strong and lasting links with company "stakeholders" who can support that strategy. Both these efforts require leadership over the long term.

The concept of sustainable development itself requires a long-term view before it makes any sense at all. It is meaningless if viewed on only a quarter-by-quarter basis. Considered in terms of generations, it is compelling, as "progress" that cannot be sustained is likely to be disastrous a few generations hence.

The concept of leadership is much discussed in books on business and industry. Perhaps this is because it is becoming less clear who really leads companies in an era of large stakes by various investment funds and of rapid mergers and takeovers. The leader—whether chief executive officer (CEO), chairman, or individual owner—must have an idea of the path the company should follow. This is the "corporate vision"—perhaps the most difficult part of the process. The vision must be refined and fleshed out so that its holder is certain it is correct; this process provides the determination needed for leadership.

The vision must then be communicated to those important to its realization in a manner both clear and motivating. The leader's actions will have to be consistent with the vision over time, to provide credibility.

It is the notion of "over time" that raises the problem of short versus long term, a problem both deeply philosophical and very practical. Not only is there no simple answer to the short-versus-long dilemma, but any attempt at a simple answer would be a dangerous exercise. In business, there can be no long term without the short term. A business that takes a year off from worrying about quarterly reports to focus on the next decade is unlikely to have a next decade.

Like most other human concerns, the problem boils down to a question of balance, and of creating a healthy tension between short and long term—so that hasty actions taken to deal with immediate issues are always examined with a view to their long-term effects. Likewise, long-term strategies must always be examined in terms of their more immediate impacts.

In some business sectors, the importance of the long term is taken for granted. If a pharmaceuticals company is not investing a reasonable amount in research and development (R&D), which decreases present profits without producing a new product for perhaps a decade, then stock market analysts will be concerned. The same is true of the money spent on exploration by minerals companies. In fact, there is evidence that the share prices of a respected company rise when it announces new R&D projects. We expect that in time investments in eco-efficiency will be regarded in the same manner—basic necessities of doing business, and investments that improve company value.

But in the meantime, some company directors defend an overemphasis on the short term by mentioning their fiduciary duty to shareholders to maximize returns. Of course, directors' first responsibility is to those who have put money in the business. But that responsibility itself is long as well as short term; it includes protecting the long-term interests of stockholders, many of whom have taken a stake they intend to hold for decades. "Fiduciary responsibility" does not automatically push leaders toward short-termism. It could be argued that it pushes them toward a view of their responsibility to both present and future stockholders.

One recent survey of British companies concluded that, on this issue, the conversation between companies and the financial markets is a "dialogue of the deaf," adding:

The perception within companies is that their discussions with investors lead them to neglect long-term strategies in the interests of immediate financial returns. Investors are perceived as placing a relatively low priority on business fundamentals—such as company loyalty, investment in people and supplier relationships—which will determine long-term success.

The perception within the investment community is that companies are preoccupied with immediate returns and are reluctant to volunteer information about the fundamentals. . . .

Ironically, many of the business leaders who complain about the short-termism of fund managers are themselves trustees of pension funds. A key test of their commitment [to a long-term approach] will be the terms of reference and time scales they set for the managers of those funds.[1]

In fact, one of the more widely accepted ways of valuing companies focuses on a longer view. This is the shareholder value analysis, which is based on free cash flows over various future forecast periods. Many surveys have found that free cash flows are a more accurate indicator of a company's value on financial markets than other indicators based on traditional formulas such as earnings or cash flow multiples.[2]

For those interested in details, the system works as follows. The free cash flow of a forecast period is composed of the earnings before interest and taxes, minus taxes, plus depreciation less capital expenditures and increases in net current assets. The estimated free cash flows (including the terminal value at the end of the explicit forecast period) get discounted to a present value that represents the total value of the company. One must deduct the debt from this total company value to arrive at what remains left to shareholders (shareholder value). Despite all the mathematics involved, the calculation of future free cash flows still requires a lot of estimates.

The point is that under this approach, some 60–80 percent of the shareholder value is reckoned for periods beyond the short term—say, beyond the next five years. Shareholder value is thus a forward-looking model that offers an indication of the long-term success of a company. Neither past nor present achievements are the prime parameters for calculating the company value (as is the case with most traditional valuation methods). First and foremost, the long-term impact of a company's strategies are being captured.

The shareholder value concept is widely accepted in the Anglo-Saxon world and has been gaining acceptance in continental Europe. One recent survey found that the discounted cash flow (DCF) model was the only approach able to capture both returns and growth: "We recently applied the DCF model to about thirty companies, using forecasts from the Value Line Investment Survey, and found very strong correlation with the companies' market value. Although these results are not scientific, they are consistent with our experience that DCF is very good at explaining companies' market value."[3]

To round off the short-term, long-term discussion, it is worth noting that today most major corporations develop longer-term views than most governments, which have a hard time looking beyond the next election. This more forward-looking approach can have a helpful, steadying influence on governments as they set sustainable development policies. Also, business has a deeper understanding of markets than governments do. So it is not only appropriate that companies become involved in developing public policies for the control of pollution and the management of resources, it is crucial that they do so.

Motivation for an Eco-efficiency Strategy

Having argued that long-term planning is an appropriate activity for those running companies, we now consider why a corporate leader might be motivated to pursue a long-term strategy of increasing eco-efficiency.

There are many reasons for such motivation. Individually, any single one of the reasons listed here might be dismissed as unconvincing.

Their power lies in the summation of the parts. In many parts of the world:

- regulations are getting tougher and, more important, enforcement is getting tougher;
- more use is being made of economic instruments to encourage constant improvement;
- banks are more willing to lend to cleaner companies;
- insurers are more willing to insure cleaner companies;
- investors are increasingly interested in investing in cleaner companies;
- the best and the brightest are more willing to work for cleaner companies;
- "green consumerism" is maturing and switching from brand loyalty to company loyalty, with the general public believing it has a growing right to have a say in what companies do;
- the search for eco-efficiency can motivate a company and its employees to become more innovative on many fronts;
- eco-efficiency is an excellent avenue for introducing the concept and the practice of Total Quality Management (which logically must include environmental quality in terms of eco-efficiency);
- media coverage of pollution and environmental liability problems is becoming more sophisticated—and thus harder for companies to shrug off; and
- many relatives of company directors (spouses, children) are becoming more concerned and sophisticated about environment and social issues.

A U.N. poll of multinationals found that 86 percent of respondents listed laws (actual and impending) and 90 percent listed market opportunities as the biggest influences in "their moving towards sustainability." Next came the company's national government (79 percent) and employees (74 percent).[4]

Another survey of multinationals, this one by *The Economist*, offered a long list of examples of successful companies involved in eco-efficiency and community development activities: western chemical companies are becoming extremely vigilant in policing the industry to

decrease pollution scandals; computer companies are pus
higher environmental standards; accountancy firms are helping po
communist countries set up modern accounting systems; and oil companies are guaranteeing to build schools and airports and act as "green
watchdogs" in return for drilling rights.[5] All these activities are so
obviously investments in present and future business that, the survey
concludes, "it seems that behaving like good corporate citizens makes
eminent business sense."

In 1995, British Petroleum (BP) reported that the previous year it had
spent $29 million on community projects including education, environ-
mental improvement, and various types of community development,
such as road-building.[6] BP recently formed a partnership with the
World Bank to do community work in the poor, rural region of Colombia where a consortium of oil companies is developing large oil
fields. During the early nineties, the big multilateral development
banks and U.N. agencies expressed a growing desire to work with
business on sustainable development issues. Some companies have
reciprocated the interest. But there is such a deep cultural rift between
business and these big agencies that these working partnerships are
extremely rare.

The *Economist* poll also noted that multinationals tend to help the
countries in which they operate by imposing international standards
wherever they go—"or have them imposed on them by global shareholders and the media. On the whole they find it easier to operate one
set of rules everywhere around the world, rather than to apply different rules in different places. So multinationals clamour for more
global—and usually higher—standards partly because it makes their
lives easier, partly because it imposes the same standards on their
competitors."[7]

It might seem odd to list increasingly tough regulations as a reason
for moving toward eco-efficiency at a time (at this writing) when the
U.S. Congress seems bent on tearing apart that nation's pioneering
environmental regulatory structure. It is impossible to know how this
will turn out. But strangely, this pressure could turn out to be a good
thing for the U.S. environment. Americans have enjoyed a relatively
healthy environment for so long now that they take it for granted and
often resist paying the costs—whether those be taxes, charges, or the

inconvenience of separating rubbish and recycling. The present debate in the United States offers them the choice of paying less and returning to the era of polluted rivers, lakes, and skies, or developing a more efficient and cost-effective regulatory policy than at present. It is no bad thing occasionally to face tough choices over benefits taken for granted; it can help a nation reexamine priorities.

The "family pressure" trend listed above raises an odd sort of observation that must be made: company leaders are human beings and often allow themselves to appear so. Other financial-market players—analysts, auditors, raters, actuaries—tend to strive to appear to be driven by nothing but bottom-line considerations. As anyone reading the business pages knows, company directors are more willing than others to talk about values, beliefs, and ideals. Many successful CEOs labor to achieve various value-driven, non-bottom-line goals—such as increased employee participation, more employee ownership, and eco-efficiency—without damaging the bottom line.

The "green consumerism" in the list also deserves comment. Consumers have become cynical about paying extra for brands advertised as "green." Instead, "the critical focus is shifting away from brands and towards companies which should be seen to be driving, not jumping on, the environmental bandwagon," says social anthropologist Franceska van Dijk.[8] "Opportunities exist for credible companies to communicate about the environment not as a sales bid but as an integral part of corporate responsibility, high quality service and customer care," she notes. "Competitively, corporate environmental sensitivity can be seen as a 'high level discriminator'—one of the elements which make up the portrait of the company and how it does business, and one whose influence on the perceptions of stakeholders is growing."

An increasing number of books contain case studies showing that eco-efficiency improves the bottom line by cutting the costs of resources and of compliance and by savings through other forms of efficiency.[9] But there seems to be a general suspicion among some directors that all these are "special cases." In a debate on these issues one executive was heard to mutter: "It is all right for 3M to prove that 'Pollution Prevention Pays'; they make sticky tape. But it is harder to prove it if you are running an oil refinery or a steel mill." (Actually, 3M produces tens of thousands of different and rapidly changing products, so it is always having to face new pollution challenges. It is, however, easier for a company like 3M, with a rapid turnover of capital base caused by rapid development of new products, to invest in eco-efficiency than it is for a steel, primary chemicals, or cement company, which changes plant and equipment more slowly, to do so.)

Yet it is a commonplace to say that good management is crucial to corporate success. Good housekeeping, compliance with environmental laws, and efficiency in general are all tests of good management. All are part of Total Quality Management. So it is easy to believe that efforts toward eco-efficiency can help to improve management systems and functions.

But can anyone prove it?

Until very recently, not enough public information on companies' environmental performances has been available even to attempt such a proof. In many countries, such data are still secret and unavailable. But in the United States, recent publications of emissions and other performance indicators are making such studies possible.

In 1994, Stuart Hart and Gautam Ahuja of the University of Michigan examined 127 Standard & Poor's (S&P) 500 firms in manufacturing, mining, or some type of production.[10] They produced a variable called "emissions reduction," based on the Investor Responsibility Research Center's (IRRC) 1993 Corporate Environment Profile. Then it was easy to seek correlation between decreases in emissions and an improved "bottom line." They found that return on sales and return on assets began to improve significantly the year after a major reduction in emissions.

It took about two years for an effect to be seen on return on equity (ROE). The authors speculate that this could be because poor environmental performance may affect a firm's cost of capital. This effect is likely to cause the longer time lag in ROE improvement since it requires that the market become aware of the firm's environmental performance and reflect this in the cost of capital, and that the firm raise capital at this new cost level.

The study also reached the not-unexpected conclusion that the biggest polluters enjoyed the greatest bottom-line benefits in cleaning up. Yet it suggests that even relatively clean companies can profit from the effort.

A similar study in 1995—in the form of a working paper at this writing—by the IRRC itself used U.S. government data to divide all S&P 500 firms into "high" and "low" polluters—based on such variables as litigation, fines, toxic emissions, size of chemical spills, and so on—and then tracked the stock market results of these two "portfolios."[11]

The authors concluded that:

Overall, the study found no penalty for investing in a "green" portfolio and, in many cases, low pollution portfolios achieved better returns than high pollution packages and the S&P 500 index. The study suggests that the increasing attention being paid to environmental management issues by both corporations and investors may well be warranted from the perspective of financial self-interest.

They also noted that "little if any of the information on environmental performance used in this study was available in any systematic manner until recently." This supports our general belief that increased and improved information may be one of the most important factors encouraging financial markets to value eco-efficiency.

Both sets of authors noted that although they had found a correlation between increased eco-efficiency and improved financial results, they had not proved cause-and-effect. Causality might run "backwards," in the sense that increasingly profitable firms might have more money to invest in eco-efficiency. However, according to Hart and Ahuja, "our hunch is that a 'virtuous circle' exists. . . . That is, firms can realize cost savings and plow those savings back into further emission reduction projects for a number of years before the investments/savings balance turns negative."[12]

Many more such studies were in the pipeline as of this writing. But in the meantime a number of the leading companies are beginning to make a leap of faith and claim that eco-efficiency is good for them. Typical is Dow Europe in its *Environmental Progress Report 1993:* "We have come to recognize that Dow's long-term financial health is directly related to its environmental performance. Environmental improvements lead to increased productivity, quality and reliability. They create value for our customers. Environmental improvement is and will continue to be a point of strategic differentiation for Dow."[13] According to Monsanto's 1991 *Environment Annual Review:* "Monsanto's ability to develop new products, enter new markets, sell our current products and operate our manufacturing facilities profitably depends upon continuous improvement in environmental performance."[14]

As for the more difficult social side of sustainable development, there is even evidence that corporate activity in this field can help the bottom line. A report from the British group Action: Employees in the Community argues that companies gain business benefits by encouraging employees to sit on the boards of community organizations.[15] These benefits include awareness of demographic, policy, or other trends that can affect the market; an understanding of business opportunities in community areas such as health, education, and housing; feedback on company reputation and performance; and contacts with customers, potential partners, opinion formers, and investors.

A number of companies use community and charity assignments as part of their management training programs. It has been claimed that this approach is very helpful in the age of the "de-layered company," as it gives junior staff varied challenges and a taste of responsibility when there is no longer a corporate ladder to climb. The value of this training approach is hotly debated, and a number of large British companies that believe in it have been trying to develop ways of measuring its effectiveness.[16]

The Counterview

There are, of course, other sides to the arguments that eco-efficiency pays and that good companies are cleaning up for sound business reasons. Simply stated, they are that eco-efficiency does not pay and that a few big companies are driving up environmental standards to squeeze out less well capitalized competitors.

The other general negative view is that whatever business leaders say, everything they do in the environment field is driven by regulations—if not actual regulations, then the threat or implied threat of regulations. Some believe that this is what is really behind much of business's self-regulation and "voluntary standards."

This debate was most visible in 1994 in the pages of the *Harvard Business Review* after two McKinsey consultants published an article entitled "It's Not Easy Being Green," in which they offered examples of companies achieving "win-win" cleanup solutions and then concluded it was all very unrealistic, that environmental costs were skyrocketing, and that few companies see any economic paybacks from their environmental investments.[17] Little direct evidence for these conclusions was cited, aside from a 1991 McKinsey international survey of CEOs that found that most expected environmental spending to double as a percentage of sales during the nineties. They also offered the example of an unnamed company that had spent too much on the environment to the detriment of other projects. The *Review* asked 12 experts to offer their own views on the topic in the next issue.[18]

Frances Cairncross, who until recently covered the environment for *The Economist*, maintains that it is positively dangerous for politicians and management gurus like Michael Porter to claim that cleaning up improves competitiveness, as this may disappoint industrialists.

"The best policies to improve competitiveness certainly do not involve tougher environmental regulation," she wrote in her recent book.[19] "A cleaner environment is worth having for its own sake, and industry is more likely to help to deliver it if politicians do not oversell the case for high environmental standards." This is a rare example of a journalist expressing concern that naive industrialists are being led astray by overenthusiastically green politicians.

The chaos of this debate allows us, indeed requires us, to make our position clear. We nowhere claim that tougher regulations improve a company's or a country's competitiveness. In fact, given the ad hoc way in which regulations have proliferated, we have called for a pruning back until the ones that are left are necessary, transparent, evenly applied, and cost-effective. We have argued that more could be achieved with well-constructed economic instruments, including improvements in the competitiveness of eco-efficient companies.

Such instruments pose difficulties for business leaders that are rarely discussed openly. Both the Business Council for Sustainable Development and the International Chamber of Commerce have welcomed their judicious use. But business/environment writer John Elkington points out that the market can be a much harsher master than governments: "Markets are much less susceptible to the sort of industry lobbying which slows down the passage of new laws and blunts their enforcement."[20] He adds that in a market-based system, "a company's day of judgment can come out of the blue, with its share price plummeting or its customers switching almost overnight to alternative suppliers." Thus a number of corporate directors, although they would rarely admit it, actually favor government regulations over market instruments. They have learned to deal with the former but not the latter. This division is an issue that business will have to work out frankly and openly.

We have never been so bold as to claim, to borrow a Dow Chemical slogan, that "Waste Reduction Always Pays." As we pointed out in the first chapter, it is hard to make eco-efficiency pay when the prices of resources are too low, including those resources called "sinks," into which waste is discarded: air, ground, rivers, and oceans. Neither can eco-efficiency pay if it is driven too much by illogical gusts of regulation and too little by sound, systemic mixes of regulation, market instruments, and self-regulation. A study by DuPont has shown how much waste reduction can be achieved for relatively little outlay if companies approach the task on the basis of cost-effectiveness.[21] Our main argument is that, driven by the many forces we have outlined above, including a push from farsighted business leaders, the world is moving toward market frameworks that reward eco-efficiency more systematically than it is rewarded today. Smart companies will help this happen and be ready when it does.

As for the companies already driving up standards by their superior performance and thereby making it tough on others, this is called competition. It happens in open markets, and we are in favor of it.

Communicating the Strategy

Once a strategy is devised—whether for eco-efficiency or anything else—it must be communicated to all stakeholders. Business is usually better at talking about the need to communicate than doing it. A good deal of business communication struggles so hard to be very simple and very positive that it falls into the traps of being simplistic and saccharin. There are dangers in communicating an eco-efficiency strategy, in that the concept is ever so slightly complex and it requires a few statements that are not good news—such as the fact that the company is not already as eco-efficient as it should be.

Communicating long-term strategy is also more inherently difficult in that long-term aspects tend to be more difficult to evaluate and define. Uncertainty, variability, and margins of error obviously increase with time, while predictability and calculability decrease. This means that the longer the time horizon of a decision's impact, the more leaders must offer their own personal assessments and value judgments in place of plain quantitative analysis and calculations.

So communication begins at the highest level of responsibility, and it must respect both the company culture and the scenarios for the future of its economic, social, and natural environments. Communication both within the company and with its stakeholders is essential during the decision-making process and after a decision has been made, to motivate people to move toward the established long-term goal.

Leaders must be both very forceful and very careful in communicating their strategies. If they are, they can bring the markets along with them on investments that pay back only over long periods. Care is required not only in being clear and accurate about the present situation and plans for the future, but also in not going to extremes of either under- or overenthusiasm. Some companies have moved from saying as little as possible about the environment to the other extreme of emphasizing how much they are spending on it. Consider the following:

The amount of capital spent [by Union Pacific Corporation] on environmental matters has increased substantially. For example, capital expenditures from 1990 through 1992 grew from $4.4 million to $12.2 million for pollution prevention projects and from $24.2 million to $38.5 million for remediation activity.[22]

Surely stakeholders, including stockholders, deserve a more sophisticated message than "we are spending millions on the environment." This is particularly true as the more sophisticated stakeholders realize that companies with high environmental expenditures might simply be very dirty rather than very eco-friendly.

And money spent on the environment is not necessarily money well spent, a fact environmentalists are hesitant to point out. In 1993, DuPont compared and ranked 700 different waste reduction initiatives.[23] The ranking system combined net present implementation costs with the lifetime emission reductions by weight for all projects.

It also separated projects into "efficient" and "marginal" categories, making it much easier to identify and support those that were the most beneficial. The exercise revealed that the cost per pound of waste reduced by a specific initiative can vary by as much as five orders of magnitude across the company. Reducing one pound of waste can cost as little as a penny or as much as $1,000. DuPont also found that 80 percent of possible environmental benefits can be achieved in the first 20 percent of projected costs, when initiatives are undertaken in order of their cost-effectiveness.

"By examining this result, business leaders can see why some of their projects are considered marginal from the overall corporate point of view, and others, which might be less important to them, demonstrate better cost-to-benefit performance, and are therefore more desirable in terms of meeting a corporate goal," wrote the DuPont project manager. "The result is also some hard evidence to back up the commonly held belief that regulatory work is more expensive than voluntary measures. DuPont's analysis shows that on average, regulatory-driven work costs more than three times as much as voluntary reduction for the same environmental benefit."

So there are eco-<u>in</u>efficient ways of moving toward eco-efficiency. Managers have to persuade stakeholders not only that they are moving efficiently in the right direction, but that they are exercising the same degree of financial prudence in pursuing eco-efficiency as they would exercise in pursuing market share.

Although we deal with company environmental reporting elsewhere (see chapter 7), it is worth offering the example here of the Baxter company (which deals with global medical products). This firm produces a separate profit and loss account on its environmental performance. A recent Baxter environmental performance report states that:

Baxter reported sales of $8.9 billion in 1993. . . . Savings reaped from the environmental program in 1993 amounted to $48.3 million. Cumulative savings for air toxics reductions and packaging reductions were $42 million and $25 million since 1988 and 1990, respectively. Costs for compliance, remediation and waste disposal were $24.8 million. This means savings reaped from our proactive environmental program in 1993 were $23.5 million net of all estimated costs and capital expenditures. That amounts to eight cents per share towards Baxter's profitability. . . . Over \$14 million in opportunities for future cost savings have been identified. Baxter's \$24.8 million expenditure is 0.3 percent of its 1993 sales. This is considerably less than the average of two percent of sales which 220 companies reported spending in a survey conducted in 1991 by Booz Allen and Hamilton.[24]

Here is a company able to say not only how much it is spending but how much it is saving through eco-efficiency. Such reports also increase the value on the financial markets of clean companies.

Much has been written recently about companies' needs to consider in their decision-making process the concerns of a wider circle of stakeholders. This simply means that a company recognizes as participants in its activities not only the obvious and oft-discussed individuals—shareholders, employees, and customers—but also the less obvious: neighbors, citizen groups, suppliers, and government at all levels. The motivation for doing so is not to "do good" but to do better business. In *Changing Course*, we offered a number of detailed examples of how this process actually helped companies be more effective and efficient.[25] Benefits include:

- increased employee support,
- improved morale,
- better policy advice,
- greater public acceptance of corporate activity,
- reduced risk and liability (as stakeholders provide early warning),
- more self-regulation and less government regulation, and
- increased confidence of regulators that the business is in compliance.

Another way of looking at this is to focus more on a company's key relationships and less on its profit-and-loss results. This may at first sound either too radical or too New Age naive. But it is really just basic common sense. The bottom line depends on a business's key relationships—with customers, suppliers, media, the general public, neighbors, and government. To worry first about the number and only then about the people is like a football team manager worrying first about the scores and only then about the team, the coaches, the trainers, and the fans. In business, it is important to remember which determines what, and it is the relationships that ultimately determine the bottom line.

A recent survey of British companies offered three reasons for British business lagging behind the competition in many other nations: "complacency and ignorance of global standards" (failure to build international relationships), "over-reliance on financial measures of performance" (rather than focusing first on stakeholders), and "our national adversarial culture" (being quicker to face off adversaries—such as environmental critics and perhaps disgruntled suppliers—than to build strong partnerships).[26] The survey and report argued throughout for more of a relationship-based approach and—more important—for the inclusion of more relationships, particularly with the sorts of stakeholders we have mentioned. It also found that there was an overlap in relationships, such that customers could not be treated one way and employees another; there is a strong correlation between customer loyalty and employee loyalty.

The nature of business relationships varies a great deal from culture to culture. In the United States and the United Kingdom, banks are discouraged from owning large stakes in companies, and there are more small private shareholders and mutual and pension funds. Thus companies tend to have a politely adversarial relationship with their bankers and are more concerned about shareholders. This system provides a flexibility that can relocate capital quickly and efficiently as conditions change. The Japanese and German systems, in which large stakes are held by banks and—in the Japanese case—by other corporations, provide lower-cost direct monitoring of managers. But this approach also decreases transparency in the markets and makes them more unwieldy and less liquid. In being encouraged to focus on a few big stakeholders, companies in these countries are not good at working with a wider circle of stakeholders.

In a report published by the Bank for International Settlements, Stephen Prowse suggested that each system might benefit from moving toward an environment "that allows market forces a greater role in determining which is the optimal method of corporate control for a particular firm."[27] In Anglo-Saxon countries, this would mean relaxing constraints on big investors taking large, active stakes. Japan and Germany would open their corporate securities markets, something already happening. The same logic would apply in nations such as France and Italy, which are considering new ways of organizing their financial markets.

In the "post-socialist" parts of the globe, entire systems of stakeholder relationships must be either rebuilt or constructed from scratch,
as previously there were no shareholders, or investment banks, or
strong citizens' groups. The approach that has received most of the
media attention is the various schemes to give away vouchers for
shares in formerly state-owned companies. Another type of stakeholder solution gaining attention in these countries is the partial ownership of firms by their employees (not the same thing as
co-operatives, wherein employees tend to own the whole firm, usually
with equal shares).

Jeffrey Gates spent eight years working for the U.S. Senate Finance
Committee drafting laws to encourage employee stock ownership
plans (ESOPs). Today more U.S. employees are enrolled in ESOPs than
belong to labor unions. Gates argues forcefully that capitalism is effective at producing capital but less effective at producing capitalists.[28]
Thus the majority of people are connected to the economic systems in
which they operate by only the very fragile thread of a job and its
salary. He argues that this situation is bad for the worker and bad for
the economic system, in that it creates a growing gap—and growing
tension—between the capitalists and the job holders. Increased employee ownership would not only improve corporate governance, it
would produce a larger pool of people—often neighbors—who have
a more structured say in their companies' environmental and eco-
efficiency activities.

Gates's various "ownership re-engineering" schemes go beyond the
individual company, however. He also suggests that customers of, say,
a power company or a water company become part owners—in ways
entirely in keeping with the spirit of capitalism. This automatically
produces greater stakeholder participation in these environmentally
important companies.

Professor Michael Porter, in an article on improving investment
patterns rather than stakeholder relationships, came up with recommendations of interest in a discussion of long-term stakeholder participation in companies.[29] These included:

• modify corporate-ownership structures by removing restrictions on
share ownership, reducing tax barriers on private owners holding
significant stakes, and encouraging long-term employee ownership;

- create an incentive for long-term equity investment by eliminating restrictions on banks holding equity in companies and reducing subsidies for investment in property; and

- improve the relationships between owners, lenders, and management by loosening restrictions on institutional board membership, encouraging representation by major customers, suppliers, financial advisers, employees, and community representatives.

(Porter also argued for modifications in existing corporation law to make long-term shareholder value rather than current stock price the appropriate corporate goal, a recommendation that has a bearing on discussions here about valuing companies.)

Companies are gradually becoming more effective at communicating with their various stakeholders through different tools developed or redesigned for the purpose, such as environmental progress reports, annual reports, community advisory committees, roundtables, sponsorships, company executives' work on neighborhood organizations, and information kits.

The leading companies are doing it, and they are finding that it pays off. But reaching all the stakeholders with a unified, convincing, consistent, motivating message requires unity of vision at the very top of the company.

Ways Forward

It is hard to suggest globally appropriate ways forward for business leaders because—although financial markets are slowly developing a globally homogenous culture—business culture remains specific to different countries and regions.

Suffice it to say that eco-efficiency remains at present a minority concern everywhere. Thus leaders who see it as a worthwhile pursuit will want to join one of the many local, national, regional, or global business and environment or business and sustainable development organizations springing up everywhere. This can lead not only to better understanding of issues and eventually to better policies, but also to new business partnerships and opportunities.

Company directors should seek new ways to cooperate with governments in several areas. One is the raising of environmental standards, ensuring that they are respected, and the creation of environment-enhancing financial instruments that work for business. Another is to examine some of the new public-private funding mechanisms to create new business opportunities, as discussed in chapter 2. Traditionally, companies' main contacts with government involved negotiating over regulations and taxes, and lobbying for individual favor. The time has come for business to create or join business organizations that form new partnerships with government to build a policy framework that promotes and rewards eco-efficiency.

Back in the company, a system needs to be established to foster the processes described here as constituting leadership: developing a coherent vision, communicating it to stakeholders, examining key relationships and measuring their health, developing a reward system for those furthering the corporate vision, and carefully monitoring trade-offs between short-term actions and long-term strategies.

As the market becomes a tougher judge of a company's eco-efficiency than government officials are, company leaders will want to have their strategies in place, their teams trained and fit, and their stakeholders loyal.

The Investors and Analysts

When corporations treat the environment badly, they treat their investors badly. The fiscal health of our pension funds is the absolute measure for any decision we make. We can never endanger the check of a beneficiary. That is why we will not tolerate endangerment to our portfolio due to corporate environmental carelessness.

H. Carl McCall, New York State
Comptroller and sole trustee of the
New York State & Local Retirement Systems, 1995

The four-page letter that landed on the desks of 275 fund managers in the City of London on August 6, 1993, stood out from the rest of the paper that washed over their desks that busy Friday.[1] It recommended a boycott of a $250-million share offer in one of the world's biggest makers of plywood, Barito Pacific of Indonesia, supported by Salomon Brothers, the respected U.S. investment bank.

"The proposed expansion of the Barito Group," said the letter from a consortium of environmental groups, "is not in the interests of the environment, large numbers of local and indigenous people, whose lands have been logged by the company without their consent, or, in the longer term, the process of sustainable development of the Indonesian economy."

London's *Financial Times* recorded the letter as the London financial markets' first taste of environmental lobbying.[2] It quoted one recipient, Simon Fraser, investment director of Fidelity Investment Services, as saying: "I've been in the business over 10 years and this is the first time I've been confronted with a situation like this. It's difficult to know how to react."

Chapter 4 Summary

What do those who study company performance and pick winners for the investors—the financial analysts—think about the environment? Not a lot, according to a poll in one of the world's top financial centers, the City of London. The survey showed that most analysts feel the bulk of environmental issues are moral or emotional and are therefore irrelevant to their job of making rational assessments. Two thirds said the subject was of no interest to their clients. Three quarters did not see the environment as a competitive issue within the business sectors they covered.

Predictable? Yes. Analysts, and the majority of investment managers, find the environment rather irksome and have tended to ignore it because of its moral connotations. But they are beginning to drop their blinkers because increasingly they find the environment cropping up as a reason for big losses in the insurance market, sizable provisions in company accounts for contaminated land, and heavy costs for water and electricity utilities struggling to meet tightening standards. They also see some of their colleagues making respectable returns in investment funds that trumpet their environmental ethics.

Maybe this is why the same survey shows that analysts think the environment will become more important in the next 10 years. If their prediction is right, it will be because others have managed to give investors what they really want: a price for the environment.

Talk to us about the environment in financial terms, say investment managers, and we'll listen. This is what is beginning to happen. Attempts are being made to provide objective environmental rating systems that will, eventually, identify both risk and opportunity for investors. Furthermore, environmental campaigners are waking up to the potential of harnessing the dormant power of shareholders and pensioners to create change in the companies or funds they collectively own.

Meanwhile, some trustees and fund managers are beginning to question the currency of nineteenth-century definitions of prudence and fiduciary duty. These exclude social and environmental concerns but still form the central pillar on which investment managers base their decisions today.

This attempt by environmental campaigners to sway the investment community failed; it left the fund managers wondering quite what had happened—and the issue oversubscribed. If a demonstration was needed that most investors and environmentalists speak different languages, the Barito letter provided it. Although the writers had tried hard to translate their concerns into arguments that financial advisers could understand, they failed to convince their audience. The *Financial Times* quoted one manager as saying: "They would do their cause more good if the language was less emotive. They use phrases like 'unacceptable political connections'. Unacceptable to whom?"

Such differences are at the heart of the debate about how investors should conduct themselves in a world that is becoming more sensitive to environmental issues and therefore, it is argued, more risky for investors. Critical to these differences is the relationship between the owners (or controllers) of investment capital and the people who are charged with investing it. The description of this relationship might be couched in management jargon of clients and advisers, but in some senses it is master-servant in nature, with a strict regulatory framework to keep the servants in line. The concern here is about the ways in which the servants—those who manage the funds for the owners and advise them on the best investment strategies—operate, and about what motivates them.

The vast majority of investment managers (that is, all the various intermediaries involved in managing investment funds) view most environmental concerns—and certainly that thing called sustainable development—as utterly irrelevant to their jobs. Such issues, unless defined by the law or given a number in the accounts, are for them simply out of play. If you want these things to be considered, say the managers, then change the rules that govern the way we operate. Otherwise, forget it, because we cannot reform the system from within.

This response is perfectly reasonable. But it ignores the changes that have already taken place in the investment sector and those that are under way. Fundamental to the change is a shift in the interpretation of the definitions that control the relationship between investment managers and the owners of investment capital—definitions of prudence and fiduciary duty, and indeed of ownership itself. These are worth exploring in greater detail.

Ownership

It used to be easy to identify the factory owner; you simply looked for the big house on the hill. Now, with the growth of share ownership and especially of pension funds, the picture is muddied. It is useful to look more closely at how this came about, at the shifts that have taken place in recent history, and at how owners are now, in most cases, far removed from the control and indeed the influence of their capital.

Not many decades ago, the major stockholders of companies were those who founded and ran the firms, along with their families, such as the Rockefellers, Vanderbilts, and Fords. Today, owner-founders are rare among the bigger companies, but still a majority among smaller enterprises.

The shift in ownership was a result of a number of different factors. Growing numbers of individuals began buying shares as the family companies went public to finance expansion. Financial reporting in newspapers became more sophisticated. Brokerage houses—whose income then was derived mainly from fees for dealing in shares—sought to expand their business by attracting more customers.

As a consequence of these developments, the ownership of companies in the sixties became widely dispersed. This led to an increase in the power of company directors, as such a diffuse group of owners could not exert many of the functions of control usually associated with ownership.

In the seventies, a new concentration process began as institutional investors—pension funds, investment (mutual) funds, insurance companies, banks, industrial companies, and others—bought more and more shares as they became richer. The assets of U.S. pension funds increased more than fourfold from 1974 to 1984, from about $30 billion to $140 billion.[3]

Private pension fund assets in the United States stood at $2.5 trillion ($2,500 billion) in 1994, up from $250 million in 1975; California's public employee pension fund alone rose from $13.3 million in 1979 to $80 billion in 1994.[4] Nationwide, pension funds own 25 percent of all stock, including some 60 percent of Standard & Poor's 500 stocks.[5]

In the United Kingdom, institutional investors own more than 60 percent of the equity of all quoted companies, corresponding to a value of about $600 billion.[6] Pension funds own 34.2 percent of the institutional total ($205 billion), insurance companies 17.3 percent ($100 billion), banks 0.6 percent ($4 billion), and investment funds 9.1 percent ($55 billion). Private investors, who in 1963 owned 54 percent, today control only 17.7 percent ($105 billion). Foreign investors own 16.3 percent ($98 billion). Among the latter, investors from the United States control about $41 billion, and EU investors about $15 billion. U.K. pension funds have increased their stake from just 6.4 percent in 1963 to more than 34 percent in 1994.

In Switzerland, pension funds manage 34 percent, insurance companies 31 percent, and banks 14 percent of the financial assets of institutional investors.[7] The total volume managed by institutional investors is estimated to be more than 800 billion Swiss francs ($600 billion) in 1994.

Obviously, institutional investors are a major force in equity markets and therefore in company ownership. What is still unclear is how they will choose to use their power, or indeed if their influence will be conscious or merely a consequence of their dominant position in the market.

An example of the effect of their power can be seen in Britain, where pension funds have invested heavily in commercial property. To maximize their investment, the funds need to reduce their risks and keep rents as high as possible. This has led, in some areas, to the demise of small businesses, such as specialist shops that can neither afford the rents nor provide the high level of security, and to the supremacy of the large chains, which can. This has consequences for consumer choices and the retail mix in shopping centers, and it reduces opportunities for small businesses.

Pension fund managers would argue, rightly, that such a change is merely a consequence of market forces; they are responsible for getting the best return for their pensioners, not for setting town-planning policies. The rights or wrongs of these market forces are not the issue here; the point is just that shifts in the control of equity do affect the markets and create consequences for the way we live, including our environment.

The financial power of pension funds is set to increase in line with the West's fast-aging population. European governments, most of which have subsidized pension plans through taxation, are beginning to encourage private plans so that their own burden can be reduced. This will be a slow process because of political sensitivities, but some observers predict that Europe's current pension fund assets of $2 trillion could quadruple by the year 2020.[8] The Netherlands and the United Kingdom, with the largest pension fund assets, are leading the way. Japan and China, which also have rapidly aging populations, could follow this trend.

As a result of a shift toward private pensions, workers and pensioners themselves could become a powerful financial force in the markets. The power will, of course, be tempered by national laws (for example, those that force a percentage of funds to be invested domestically) and by pensioners' lack of awareness of their power. But it is not unthinkable that pensioners, if suitably motivated and made aware, could pressure their fund managers into investment decisions intended to bring about positive social and environmental consequences.

Fiduciary Duty

We must minimize risk, maximize returns, and preserve capital—that is our legal duty. This is the traditional, correct view of those who manage other people's money. Such an interpretation of fiduciary duty (or trustee's duty) is at the core of arguments to exclude soft or nonfinancial factors, such as the environment or social goals, in investment decisions.

This duty is based on the notion of prudence, derived from a Massachusetts court definition in 1830, known as the "prudent man rule":

All that can be required of a trustee to invest is, that he shall conduct himself faithfully and exercise sound discretion. He is to observe how men of prudence, discretion and intelligence manage their own affairs, not in regard to speculation, but in regard to the permanent disposition of their funds, considering probable income, as well as the probable safety of the capital to be invested.[9]

The prudent man rule became part of the investment culture of the previous century, at a time when environmental issues did not concern society. While our society has changed, the "prudent man" investment culture of the nineteenth century remains dominant to this day. Change within that culture—and there has been dramatic change—has occurred within the constraints of the traditional notions of fiduciary duty, rather than during reform of it. This was one of the factors leading to the growth of financial engineering products, such as derivatives, that are even more financially pure and further removed from social or environmental concerns than are traditional market instruments, such as bonds and stocks.

Yet the financial intermediaries have not willfully ignored environmental issues. Indeed, the problems of contaminated land and the capital costs of conforming to tougher environmental laws would not be so high on the business agenda if players in the financial markets had not taken some notice. The investment managers responded to these issues because it was prudent to do so; they posed a financial risk that had to be avoided or minimized. The issues were risky because there were numbers attached and these numbers could, at times, be found in the accounts.

But what of those risks that have no numbers or prices and will not be reported—the long-term risks to the fabric that sustains us: the soil, seas, water, plants, and animals? Surely these risks should be noted by the prudent person in charge of somebody else's money, especially when that money—as in pension funds—has to work for this generation and those to come? And what about those eco-efficient companies that have improved their environmental performance and thereby reduced their threat to the environment and therefore the risk to their investors? Surely these companies are a good bet and should be rewarded with a higher share price?

These are the questions that some within the investment community have been asking. Their questioning is driven by an understanding of the broader concerns of society and, more important, by a frustration with the narrow nineteenth-century interpretation of prudence and fiduciary duty. They want prudence to describe more than just financial sustainability and they feel that the duty of fiduciaries should be to promote sustainable development rather than undermine it.

Of course, those who are questioning the tenets on which the entire investment culture is based are few in number, and their impact on that culture is, at best, slight. But the effect is noticeable, and it may signal that there is some pressure from within to reform the system. What, then, are these signals? There are two main indicators worth investigating further: so-called ethical/social funds and what we shall call socially responsible fiduciaries.

Ethical Funds

Ethical or social funds attract a lot of media attention. They exclude investment in the stocks of companies deemed to be unethical or irresponsible in favor of those they consider ethical and responsible; they also intend to deliver good financial returns. There are many variations to this definition, reflecting the ideologies and motivations of those who choose to invest in this way. Ethical funds may include environmental considerations, but there are also "environmental funds" or "green funds" that invest mainly either in companies that try to improve the environment or in those that strive not to harm it, or in some cases in both types of companies. There is no agreed definition of ethical funds, as they cover such a multitude of virtues.

The significance of ethical funds, certainly for this discussion, lies more in their influence on capital markets than in their size, which is comparatively insignificant. The £900 million ($1.4 billion) managed by ethical funds in the United Kingdom represents but 1 percent of all funds under management there.[10] The Social Investment Forum, a U.S. lobby group, claims that in the United States some $650 billion, or almost 10 percent of total U.S. investments, are managed according to ethical guidelines, but it uses a very broad definition of this term.[11]

These funds have attracted so much attention that they led to the creation in 1994 of a fund specializing in companies with an interest in tobacco, gambling, alcohol, and pornography.[12] The Maxus Investment Group in Cleveland, Ohio, set up Morgan Funshares as "the fund without the halo." Its investment manager, Jim Onorato, points out that the more people there are investing in ethical funds, the more money there is to be made from the "sin stocks."

Despite their growing popularity, ethical funds are dismissed by the mainstream investment community as an aberration. Cynics argue that they reflect the savvy of opportunists creating a niche marketing opportunity in the burgeoning fund management business rather than a shift in the concerns of capital markets. This may be partly so, but it would be wrong to dismiss their influence as a bearer of the ethical and in some cases the environmental message to the financial community. Indeed, it can be argued that the influence of these funds—on an evangelical level—has been grossly disproportionate to their size.

Borrowing heavily from the language of populist politics, environmental fund managers are proud of their acts of "engagement." This is when they talk to managers of institutions and companies about the importance of what they see as responsible behavior: investing for the greater good of society, and choosing to invest in companies with good environmental credentials. They argue that they are only able to "engage" their targets because of their credibility as players in the markets. A member of your average green pressure group, for example, would find it extremely difficult to arrange lunch with the financial director of a multinational corporation to discuss environmental performance, while the manager of an ethical fund has easier access.

"At the National Provident Institution (NPI), our team has engaged with many companies which are not in (our) green fund. . . . This is because NPI is committed to discussing the implications of the sustainable development debate with all corporations, as a long-term strategic issue," says Mark Campanale of NPI.[13]

The U.S.-based Jessie Smith Noyes Foundation, with assets of about $60 million, has found its own interesting way to "engage." It purchases shares in companies on an ethical/environmental basis, but it also gets involved in shareholder activism to "improve" the companies in which it holds equity.[14] It recently challenged Intel, a maker of computer chips, on its air pollution and the use of water in a desert region where one of its manufacturing facilities is located.[15] As of this writing, negotiations between the foundation and Intel were continuing.

There are other ways in which the managers of ethical funds create awareness and encourage what they see as responsible action by corporations and financial intermediaries. These individuals are prime targets for environmental performance reports, which companies are now beginning to produce (see chapter 7). They also encourage companies to disclose more and better environmental data because they need good information to satisfy their investors and achieve their promised objectives. In this way, they keep the issue of disclosure and transparency alive by constantly demanding environmental information from companies and government. Their specialist environmental and financial knowledge is also useful for policymakers who need advice on regulatory reform. And, of course, the interest of ethical funds in environmental technology companies—as a logical place to put their investments—plays an important role in funding such enterprises.

Whatever the significance of this influence, it remains subtle and severely limited by the size of the ethical funds. But some of the messages of the ethical funds are being carried by mainstream investors, or what we call the socially responsible fiduciary.

Socially Responsible Fiduciaries

Investors and their managers might generally conform to the customs of the investment culture and its rules, but this does not mean that they are a cohesive group. Some shareholders are demanding a greater say in the companies they "own." U.S. investors tend to be the most "activist" shareholders. In 1993, 300 shareholder resolutions were submitted, 22 percent covering environmental topics.[16] Some 60 percent of the environmental resolutions focused on corporate environmental reporting requirements as defined by the Coalition for Environmentally Responsible Economies (CERES). The rest covered issues such as toxic and radioactive waste, toxic release reporting worldwide, mining on native American lands, sustainable energy policy, and health, environment, and safety standards at work.

Over the years, the Interfaith Center for Corporate Responsibility has been an active campaigner against apartheid in South Africa and most recently for the CERES principles, a set of corporate and investment principles. Institutions such as the Council on Economic Priorities and the Investor Responsibility Research Center in the United States and Pensions and Investment Research Consultants (PIRC) in Britain provide a wide range of services on environmental and social affairs to the shareholding community.

Following the launch of the CERES principles in 1990, PIRC introduced the Environmental Investor's Code for pension funds in the United Kingdom. By 1991, the code was supported by funds under management exceeding £10 billion ($16.2 billion), and it has been instrumental in changing corporate activities such as the peat extraction policies of Fisons plc.[17]

In the United States, New York State & Local Retirement Systems (for public employees) and the California state pension fund have been particularly active shareholders. The New York group, for example, was responsible for ensuring that Exxon implemented board-level responsibility for environmental affairs in the wake of the Valdez oil spill.[18]

At issue here is the difference between the motivation behind the investment strategies of, say, a church or public employees pension fund and that of an investment bank. They all want to maximize their returns, but there will be differences in their expectations of the size of those returns and the methods used to get them.

Some pension funds, for example, appear willing to stretch their interpretation of prudence to enable them to practice what has become known as economically targeted investing. This is where the funds allocate a small portion of their portfolio to socially important areas thought too risky by others: mortgage-pools for low-cost housing, small business loans, and so on. By September 1993, more than $23 billion had been allocated to such efforts by the 20 biggest pension funds in the United States.[19]

This was, however, clearly a minority activity, as revealed in a survey by *Institutional Investor* magazine in the following year: 90 percent of the pension funds surveyed thought that such targeting was out of line with their interpretation of fiduciary duty.[20] Most of those surveyed were corporate pension funds, as opposed to public employee funds.

Among those who disagree with the narrow view of fiduciary duty is New York State & Local Retirement Systems. The trustee, who manages assets of more than $45 billion, appears to have accepted the existence of a link between the profitability of a company and the quality of its environmental management: "When corporations treat the environment badly, they treat their investors badly. The fiscal health of our pension funds is the absolute measure for any decision we make. We can never endanger the check of a beneficiary. That is why we will not tolerate endangerment to our portfolio due to corporate environmental carelessness."[21]

To say that this is a minority position among investors is a serious understatement. And it would be interesting to know the extent to which this organization is guided by this belief when issuing instructions to its fund managers.

Take a more complex recent case.[22] Some of the assets forming the pension fund of the staff of the British Post Office, British Telecom, British Coal, and ICI had been put in Edinburgh Java Trust, which specializes in investments in Indonesia. The trust invested part of the money in Barito Pacific, the Indonesian plywood company mentioned at the beginning of this chapter.

In Indonesia, according to the United Nations, almost 3 million acres (1.2 million hectares) of rain forest are cleared every year. Fauna at risk include the rhinoceros and orangutan. Barito had been fined for illegal logging in 1990, causing some investors to sell out. When the pension schemes' links with Barito were covered in the press in 1994, they were condemned by unions representing many staff with savings involved. Derek Hodgson, deputy general secretary of the Union of Communication Workers, said his members would be "appalled" at the way their money had been used. Representatives of the various union pension funds all stressed that only a fraction of 1 percent of the pension money had been invested in Barito.

Edinburgh Fund Managers, which administers the trust, said its investors were well aware that its rules did not provide for any ethical screen. Mike Balfour, director of the Edinburgh Fund Managers, wrote an open letter to investors in 1994:

Our stance as managers of the Trust is that its objective is to achieve capital growth with the objective of outperforming the Jardine Fleming Nusantara Index. Excluding the natural resources sector, which is important in Indonesia, would make this more difficult. However, we appreciate that publicity and attention from pressure groups may be embarrassing to some of our institutional shareholders, a situation we would like to avoid. . . . I would very much like to hear your views as it is of paramount importance to us that we provide shareholders with what they want and expect.[23]

Almost a year later, Balfour described the response to his request as varied. "But the general view was that our clients felt we should not invest in companies that misuse environmental resources because it is bad business. Market pressure will eventually work against such companies; their customers or their customers' customers will not put up with it. It is simply not good business to exploit resources to extinction. So we now look at the issue when we look at companies in which we invest."[24]

"Of course a lot of people get very worked up about the issues—quite rightly. But they have a slightly harder time being clear about their feelings when asked what they want in terms of investing in their best interests," he added.

The case reveals several interesting points. First, members of pension funds rarely have the faintest idea what is happening with their savings. Second, pension fund managers live by their reputations, and are easily embarrassed by pressure groups. Third, all involved parties claim that their contribution is only a small fraction. Fourth, fund managers typically claim that their main duty is to put financial interests first, that it is clear to everyone that their rules do not provide for any ethical considerations, and that they have to outperform an index.

Finally, there may be a sizable proportion of investors in any pension fund who do not want their retirement money to be used to destroy the environment on which their offspring will depend. The response of fund managers would be that such people ought to invest in ethical funds, although this option is not necessarily open to them.

Investment Managers in the Middle

Investment managers, as they repeatedly point out, are the willing servants of the owners or trustees of the funds under their management. They say: "We merely follow the trustees' instructions: be prudent and make the most of our money."

This is confirmed by Business in the Environment, a U.K. business group that promotes good environmental practice in business.[25] It has organized roundtable discussions with financial intermediaries to discover what motivates their decision making. The predictable answer has been: we deliver what our clients want. If you want to change our behavior, first change that of the client.

Change is difficult in these circumstances—as already noted—because of the interpretation of prudence and fiduciary duty. But there is another issue to consider, and that is ownership. Pensions increasingly dominate the markets, but pensioners and those investing in their pensions, who are the rightful owners of the funds, do not as yet have a collective view. They want the trustees and their designated managers to get on with the job of ensuring them a regular pension.

There is, however, some change detectable where the fund owner has a clearer identity and, possibly, a political agenda, as in the case of a local government. We have already noted the attitudes about economically targeted investment made by some U.S. public employee pension funds. In the United Kingdom, some local authorities are showing signs of moving toward what they see as more responsible investment strategies for their superannuation funds.

"The political nature of the councillor trustees, combined with pressure from members and a different legislative framework, have encouraged some local authorities to take an interest in ethical investment," says Mark Mansley, former chief analyst at Chase Investment Bank and now with Delphi International, a group of financial advisers in London.[26] "For example, Richmond [a town near London] has interrogated companies on environmental issues. Lincolnshire [a county] has decided to allocate funds to a small environmental fund. Hampshire [a county] is currently reviewing its investment policy, with particular regard to environmental investment."

Mansley, quoting Stuart Bell of Britain's Pensions and Investment Research Consultants, predicts that these signals of change could become a trend over the next few years. "Just as corporate governance (which amounts to closing the gap between investors and companies) has become an important issue in the last few years, so 'member accountability'—closing the gap between institutional investors and beneficiaries—may achieve prominence over the next few years."

If he is right, then it would mean a windfall for fund managers who are experienced at working under the restrictions of screened funds. The received wisdom, promoted by the mainstream managers, is that excluding too many options increases the risks of any investment strategy. This belief has been contested by ethical funds who claim that the downside of screening (such as a smaller pool to choose from and therefore restrictions on diversity) is compensated for by better research, positive selection, and better financial performance from environmentally sound companies. In 1993, a historical "back-test" over a 22-year period by U.S. ethical fund managers Winslow Management suggested "that the financial markets are placing a higher value on environmental responsibility."[27]

Mansley says ethical investment has received support from an unexpected source. "Quorum Capital Management, one of the City [of

London]'s leading quantitative investment mangers, recently investigated ethical investment for a client. They analysed the performance of a screened portfolio, where 29 percent of the eligible universe of companies were excluded, over five years. They found a modest outperformance over the last five years, but with significant variations."

He says Quorum was suitably impressed with its findings and was planning to launch an ethical management service for those funds who wanted it. "They are confident that the potential for achieving excess return from an ethically screened portfolio is the same as from an unscreened portfolio, as long as the screening does not exceed 60 per cent by market value," reports Mansley.

Factoring in the Environment

Quorum's confidence, if it can be supported by other mainstream managers, could reassure trustees who would support a more flexible interpretation of their fiduciary duty.

Although some are convinced by the financial benefits of ethical investing, the evidence to support such a conviction is far from overwhelming. If investment managers are going to change their established approaches—based largely on well-tested quantitative models that rely heavily on asset allocation through diversification—they are going to need much better arguments than those on offer now.

Much of the work purporting to show that good environmental performance is rewarded by the markets has been done in that part of the market where qualitative judgments are made—by analysts who talk to companies and get a feel for the quality of management and the rigor of decision making.

The responsibility for funds cascades down from the trustees and their immediate managers to specialist contract managers (such as treasury managers). All the intermediaries make quantitative decisions based on mathematical modelling: an asset allocation model will be used to create the initial spread of investment, and then each of the specialists to whom parts of the funds have been allocated will use a model to invest their particular portion.

Managers responsible for that portion of the fund invested in equities will, of course, also use a model. But when it comes to choosing specific stocks, they will rely on the knowledge of analysts who have

personal contact with the companies under consideration for investment—the only people in the long line of intermediaries to have such
contact. It is at this point—a long way away from the trustees or
owners—where qualitative decisions are made. And some of these
decisions will be based on how the analysts perceive the importance
of environmental factors in company performance.

Until this point, throughout the cascade of responsibility for the
funds, the environment is rarely considered. It is not part of the models
because it does not have a number attached to it—and without a
number, it cannot be part of a quantitative equation.

But the environment can become an issue at the point where investment decisions take on a qualitative nature—when the analysts talk to
the companies and consider a number of softer issues, such as corporate reputation and shifts in consumer markets.

So the environment could be an issue for analysts, but research
shows that it is not, or not yet. According to a recent survey of analysts
working in London's financial markets, they are not receptive to environmental performance arguments, although they admit that they
could be in the near future.[28] The poll is worth describing at some
length.

Sponsored by the company Extel Financial and the group Business
in the Environment, the survey sought opinions from 85 top analysts
working in 28 different sectors of business. Fifty-eight percent of those
replying said that "nonfinancial issues" (including the environment)
were unimportant to their clients, but a third—particularly analysts in
utilities and natural resources—said that they had received requests
from clients for information on environmental issues. Such requests
often focused on laws. Analysts under 35 were more likely to feel that
nonfinancial issues were important to their clients.

Over half of those interviewed considered themselves well informed
about the environmental aspects of their sectors, with those working
in utilities, natural resources, and derivatives feeling best informed.
Environmental issues were perceived mainly in terms of liabilities: 69
percent mentioned the financial consequences of incurring environmental liability costs, with cleanup costs featuring high among
concerns.

Sixty percent said environmental issues had affected their assessment of companies, primarily in terms of legal issues and cost liabili-

ties. Many mentioned U.S. legislation. Most claimed to be familiar with relevant laws, but less familiar with codes of conduct. With very few exceptions, environmental issues were not seen as opportunities, other than to boost public image.

Generally speaking, analysts did not concern themselves with environmental issues because they did not perceive them as relevant in assessing companies. Many mentioned the difficulty of getting good information and of quantifying financial impact; 40 percent said their clients did not care, and 42 percent complained of the lack of standardized reporting practices.

Just under half claimed they never used any source of environmental information. For the others, sources used included the media, notes in flotation prospectuses, and notes in annual reports. Half said they would not trust company figures on environmental initiatives, and only one third said current levels of disclosure and reporting on environmental issues were sufficient if these issues were ever to become an important part of everyday company assessment. Fifty-four percent said they would consider an externally verified corporate environmental report useful.

Companies' environmental policies were considered important by fewer than one in five. But there was overall agreement that environmental issues were going to become more important over the next decade. It was also generally agreed that financial analysts were not in a position to be innovative in promoting environmental protection.

The poll offers both good and bad news. Few analysts think the environment is relevant to their job, yet almost 70 percent said they understood the relevance of environmental liabilities and 60 percent said environmental issues had affected their assessment. These two figures would have been much lower a decade previously. Also, analysts think the environment is going to become more important in their business. And it is interesting that the younger ones do not say that the environment is important to the analysts themselves, but rather that it and other "nonfinancial issues" are important to their clients.

The findings can perhaps best be summed up with the thought that when environmental issues have a quantifiable financial impact (or a price), then analysts consider them important, and impacts are taken into account, despite poor data.

The emphasis here is on describing environmental impact in financial terms—giving it a price. This is clearly very difficult, as emphasized throughout this book, as long as there are no widely accepted mechanisms, such as environmental indicators or risk ratings (see chapter 8) that the financial community wants to use. The community demands hard facts rather than soft, subjective reasoning.

Attempts are being made to present environmental implications in the language that analysts can understand. One such case was produced by Mark Mansley of Delphi International.[29] He looked at the economic effects of climate change on the prospects of the carbon-fuel sector.

His report, commissioned by Greenpeace, analyzes the industry from the perspective of financial risk associated with possible changes in the face of environmental risks. Although it does not aim to provide a complete financial analysis, it is an interesting list of the sorts of concerns that more traditional analysts might miss, all of which have financial impacts.

The report argues that "policy measures to reduce the anticipated impacts of climate change could affect the oil and gas industry in a number of ways." Energy efficiency measures will reduce the demand for energy, for example, relative to that currently expected, particularly in the industrial world. The measures will increase the risk of overcapacity, and thus could put downward pressure on oil prices, compared with current expectations.

Alternative energy sources are becoming increasingly cost-competitive, Mansley notes, and will start to provide a cap on carbon-fuel prices, even without specific measures to support alternative energy. This limits the bull case for carbon-fuel investments based on the possibility of high energy prices. In addition, the introduction of a carbon tax would directly reduce the net price paid to producers over the longer term and remove a large proportion of the producer surplus.

Polluter liability risks are high throughout the industry, from drilling through production, transportation, and refining to marketing. When things go wrong the costs can be huge, as the Exxon Valdez and Piper Alpha disasters have shown. Ironically, one source of increased risks to the oil and gas industry may be coming from climate change itself:

wave heights are increasing in a number of locations, raising the risks to offshore platforms.

Mansley even argues that if third parties suffer serious losses as a result of climate change, "they may attempt to seek ways to recover some of the damages from those they see as responsible."

In some circumstances it can be argued now—with hard figures as backup—that environmental information influences the profitability of a company and should, therefore, influence investment decisions. For example, in 1992 the Swiss-based chemical maker Ciba spent 90 million Swiss francs ($66 million in 1992) worldwide on site remediation.[30] If these costs were excluded, its net profit margin would have been 0.32 percentage points higher, a considerable increase. Or if Ciba shares were traded with a profit/earning ratio of 13, then the capitalization of Ciba would be nearly 1 billion Swiss francs ($730 million) higher without these remediation costs: a capitalization about 5 percent higher.

It is possible to quantify these issues because contaminated land is at least partly defined and controlled (depending on where you are in the world) by the law, and you can usually get a quote on how much it would cost to clean up the mess. Similarly, it is possible to work out the volume of energy consumed per unit of sales, as some companies do—Ciba, again, is an example. This number means absolutely nothing to analysts in a market where energy is relatively cheap and not a significant factor in profitability. But the number could take on a greater importance if an energy or carbon tax were introduced, as has been suggested by the European Union. At that point, analysts would be able to calculate how energy consumption would affect earnings per share, and the markets could reward the efficient (or low energy cost) company with a higher share price.

These examples raise two issues of note. The first is about the importance of the framework—policy-driven or otherwise—in which companies operate and that sets prices. The second is about the primacy or otherwise of environmental issues.

Clearly, no matter how many indicators of environmental performance—such as an energy efficiency index—are supplied to the markets, they will be ignored unless immediately relevant. An energy efficiency index without a carbon tax, or a list of contaminated sites without a cleanup cost, means nothing to the markets. This is why mainstream investment managers ignore indicators—such as those on compliance and pollution—produced by researchers working for ethical funds.

The second point is that even when environmental performance could be significant to the equities markets—because it indicates coherent management and good prospects in environmentally sensitive markets—it is only one of many issues that analysts will consider. The cost of debt, for example, could be considered far more important to the markets than a sound environmental performance, as the Kemira Group of Finland discovered.

As Richard House of the *Institutional Investor* notes, Kemira, a chemicals company, has conducted itself as a model citizen and reduced its environmental risks through sound management.[31] But even with big profit increases, the markets have marked its shares down to below the issue price. This is due to unusually high interest rates charged by its bankers, which have reduced the sorts of profits it could be making.

Ways Forward

If investors in the equity markets are going to take the environment, and indeed sustainable development, more seriously, two things will have to happen.

First, the nineteenth-century definition of prudence and its impact on the interpretation of fiduciary duty will have to evolve to accommodate current social values. This can only be achieved through the courts or by a global consensus. Such a change seems unlikely in the near future.

Second, a way will have to be found to give the environment a price or a number—something the markets can understand. This can be achieved only by policy initiatives allowing, say, a wider trade in emissions certificates (as already happens in the United States), a shift in the tax regime to penalize pollution, or market mechanisms that internalize externalities and encourage efficient use of resources.

These actions will take time, efiort, and considerable consensus building. Perhaps an even more pragmatic, if no less difficult, action would be to improve the transparency of financial market flows and enhance the awareness of those many small individual owners of stakes in funds who are ill informed or even unwitting participants in the markets. Included here are all those who own shares and financial products such as life insurance and, of course, pensions. Once they are aware of their power and the effect of investment decisions taken on their behalf, they can play a far more active role in the workings of the market. Such a development would complicate the lives of company directors and financial intermediaries, but it would refresh the markets and might even help to make them an agent of change.

5 The Bankers

We will endeavour to ensure that our policies and business actions promote sustainable development: meeting the needs of the present without compromising those of the future. . . . We regard sustainable development as a fundamental aspect of sound business management.

Statement by Banks on the Environment
and Sustainable Development, 1992

Most banks in the industrial world are complex international financial service businesses offering a wide range of services—often confusingly called "products"—to a broad spectrum of clients.

Within the global banking system, there are many niches that many smaller banks have adapted themselves to—and often helped create. Banks in the former Soviet Union and other centrally controlled economies tend to be much simpler affairs. And banks in the Islamic world operate under a completely different set of principles.

Descriptions differ depending on what country a bank is in, but there are essentially four different types: commercial, investment, trust, and diversified services. The latter occasionally stands alone, but more often it is linked to a range of services offered elsewhere.

Commercial banking covers money transfer, deposits, loans and credits, letters of credit, foreign-exchange transactions, bullion trade, guarantees, and others. Not all lending is through what bankers refer to as "loans"; other forms include overdrafts and daytime exposure facilities. Most of the world's better-known banks fall into this category: taking deposits in their retail sector and making personal and commercial loans to borrowers.

Chapter 5 Summary

Commercial bankers, particularly in the industrial world, are beginning to respond to the sustainable development agenda.

Their attention was first caught by court cases in the United States in which a few banks that had loaned money to companies were held liable for those companies' cleanup costs.

In 1992, about 30 leading banks signed a "Statement by Banks on the Environment and Sustainable Development"; this said they "regard sustainable development as a fundamental aspect of sound business management" and noted that "environmental risks should be part of the normal checklist of risk assessment and management." Since then, the number of signatories has more than doubled and continues to grow.

Some banks have proved that they can save money—and attract new, young customers—by being eco-efficient in their internal operations, saving energy, paper, and transport costs.

Can banks encourage customers toward eco-efficiency? Should they? How?

If they do so, they will have customers with fewer environmental liabilities who are in a better position to repay loans. But it is difficult for banks to be cost-effective in encouraging eco-efficiency in small borrowers, and it is small enterprises that cause much of the world's environmental degradation, by sheer weight of numbers. This is particularly true in the developing world.

Investment banking mainly covers individual deals such as investment issuing transactions, shares and bonds, brokerage, mergers and acquisitions, and derivatives.

Trust banking generally entails activities linked to the management and investment of securities, such as financial analysis, portfolio management, funds, trust accounts, and others. These activities mainly cover the relationship between the banker and the saver/investor.

Diversified services include leasing, factoring, consulting, and credit cards.

The divisions between different types of banks are blurring in much of Europe as those that operate in politically liberal regimes move into new markets opened by deregulation. Large banks will invariably be active in most banking sectors, and banks are also moving into other sectors, such as insurance.

Development banks, such as the World Bank and the European Bank for Reconstruction and Development (EBRD), are designed to manage public and private-sector funds for aid and development. These organizations might be called banks, but their business is quite different from that of the commercial banks. The development banks have various forms of environmental controls—all criticized by environmentalists as often being overwhelmed by pressure to invest in a project, regardless of its environmental impact.

But these banks are moving from worries about "protecting" the environment to attempts to find business opportunities in sustainable development. The International Finance Corporation (the World Bank's private-sector affiliate) recently completed feasibility studies on venture capital funds that would invest in renewable energy and energy efficiency projects and in biodiversity-linked businesses.[1] The latter study revealed some biodiversity business opportunities in Latin America—in such areas as sustainable forestry and ecotourism—with the potential for both attractive·rates of return on investment and biodiversity protection.

The EBRD, founded more recently than the other development banks (1990), actually has written into its establishing agreement the statement that it will "promote in the full range of its activities environmentally sound and sustainable development."[2] The multilateral development banks are generally important to this discussion because of their economic and environmental influence and their exposure to political pressure.

Banks generally have far less influence in terms of their investment potential than, say, insurance companies or pension funds, although such generalizations can be misleading. Banks in some parts of the world, especially in Germany and Japan, are permitted to—and do—take large equity stakes in companies (see chapter 3). Their relationships with those companies are consequently much closer than those between borrowers and bankers in the United States, the United Kingdom, Scandinavia, and Canada, where large equity stakes are not allowed. In Britain, for example, banks only owned about 0.6 percent of the equity of all quoted companies ($4 billion) in 1994; institutional investors controlled more than 60 percent (about $600 billion).[3]

In this chapter, we focus on commercial banking, mainly the deposit, loan, and credit business.

Environmental Pressures on Banks

Banks in general—although there have been exceptions—have been slow to face up to environmental liabilities, opportunities, and responsibilities. None of the Northern bankers approached in 1991 to join the Business Council for Sustainable Development took up the invitation. They simply did not see pollution and environmental degradation as issues realistically on their agenda.

At the same time, a number of cases going through U.S. courts began to catch bankers' attention in a most dramatic way.

Under the U.S. Comprehensive Environmental Response, Compensation and Liability Act of 1980 (CERCLA, also known as "Superfund"), liability for cleanup is imposed on owners of contaminated sites. Companies threatened with such costs have gone to court, and tried to find others to share the costs, such as banks.

Superfund specifically exempts lenders from being classed as "owners"; but there are excepting circumstances, and several U.S. court cases have eroded this protection. The following tales, although complicated, are worth reporting because they suggest the complexity of Superfund court battles and of banks' potential liabilities, which are caused by their either operating, owning, or participating in the management of a contaminating business or aiding and abetting in environmental violations. Although these are U.S. cases, they can affect foreign banks operating in the United States.

In the Mirabile case of 1985, Turco Coatings Inc. (TCI) obtained loans from the Small Business Administration (SBA), a government agency, from Mellon Bank (MB), and from American Bank and Trust (ABT), each at a different time and for a different purpose.[4] ABT secured its loan with a mortgage on TCI real estate. TCI went bankrupt and ABT, with the Bankruptcy Court's approval, foreclosed on the mortgage and then acquired the property at a sheriff's sale. Four months later, without having actually taken title to the real estate, ABT assigned its bid to the Mirabile family, who became actual owners of the property. ABT had never operated the business, but it did secure the building against vandalism, show the property for sale, and look into the costs of storing hazardous material in barrels on the property.

The SBA secured its loan with a second mortgage. MB's loan was secured by inventory and assets; it had no interest in the real estate. After bankruptcy, however, MB's representatives often went to the property, monitored cash accounts, made sure that receivables went into the correct account, set up a reporting system between TCI and MB, required certain sales efforts, and ordered changes in management and operational procedures.

After the Environmental Protection Agency (EPA) discovered hazardous substances on the property, it began to clean up the site and sued the Mirabiles under Superfund to recover costs. The Mirabiles brought the three lenders into the suit. All three claimed exemption under Superfund.

The court held that ABT's foreclosure and limited activities were consistent with the actions of a secured lender. The SBA was also cleared of liability because it had not foreclosed on the property and not been involved in the management or operation of the business. But the court ruled that MB, despite having no interest in the real estate, was liable because it had been sufficiently involved in the day-to-day operations of TCI to make it an operator under Superfund.

In another case a year later, Maryland Bank and Trust (MBT) was held liable for cleanup because of "ownership" of a contaminated site.[5] It had loaned money to a waste management company that had allowed the dumping of hazardous waste on the property. The company defaulted on its loan and MBT, which held a mortgage on the property, foreclosed. It bought the property at a sheriff's sale. Eventually the EPA cleaned up the site and sued MBT. The court held that MBT was owner and operator of the site under Superfund, partly because the bank had held title for four years. The court warned lenders that they are deemed to be sophisticated business people who are in a position to investigate and discover potential environmental problems on their secured properties. If they fail to do so, Superfund will not absolve them of this responsibility.

A more famous case, under the "participation in management" heading, is that of Fleet Factors Corporation (FFC), a bank, in 1990.[6] In 1979, FFC had advanced funds to Swainsboro Print Works Inc. (SPWI) against the assignment of SPWI's accounts receivable. In 1976, as collateral for those advances, FFC obtained a security interest in all of SPWI's fixtures, equipment and inventory, and plant. After SPWI filed for bankruptcy (1979) and discontinued operations at the plant (1981), FFC continued to collect on the accounts receivable, under a bankruptcy court agreement. In 1982, FFC foreclosed on its interest in some of the inventory and equipment and hired another firm to auction them off. This firm spilled some hazardous chemicals located on the property. After the usual EPA/Superfund process, the court ruled that when FFC foreclosed and brought in the other firm, it was acting as operator of the facility.

Later the same year, however, another court ruled in the case of *U.S. v Bergsoe Metal Corp* that a party holding a security interest in a contaminated property could not be considered a "potentially responsible party" unless it actually participated in managing the contaminated collateral.[7] In 1991, the U.S. Supreme court refused to resolve the apparent conflict between the Fleet Factors and Bergsoe Metal cases, leaving lenders confused as to standards of practice in the United States.[8]

In an "aiding and abetting" environmental damage situation, the court may hold a bank potentially liable if, knowing environmental problems existed, it failed to condition a loan on the borrower's remedying the known problems.

These cases, though all U.S.-based, were a source of concern for the Northern banking community in general, partly because almost any development in the United States seems eventually to reach the rest of the world. Shortly after the Fleet Factors ruling, a survey by the American Bankers' Association found that 62.5 percent of U.S. commercial banks had rejected loan applications because of the possibility of inheriting environmental liability.[9] And 45.8 percent of them had by then discontinued altogether financing environmentally risky sectors, such as gasoline stations and chemical plants. Although impressive, these figures are also misleading, for they reflect the reactions of small state banks and small "savings and loan" operations, not necessarily the big players. Also, the United States is still a more litigious nation than most others, and banks elsewhere have not reacted this way.

A survey of 90 international banks in all parts of the globe found that four fifths of these leading commercial and investment institutions perform some degree of environmental financial risk assessment of borrowers before lending.[10] Fewer than half build environmental liability into their loan contract terms or monitor risks after the loan is made. But virtually all believe that the environment is going to become more important to them over the coming 15 years and will be increasingly integrated into core business activities.

European bankers have become more concerned over such liabilities since the European Commission issued a discussion paper in 1993 on "Remedying Environmental Damage," which began looking for new ways of assigning cleanup liability and costs.[11] At a hearing on the issue in late 1993, environmental groups urged that the banks should have more potential liability.[12] Most of the governments advised the Commission to stay out of the issue entirely, as it was both too complex and too mired in the different legal systems of the various countries. The Commission has shown little evidence of agreeing with either environment groups or governments, and was planning another statement on the issue in 1995.

European banks have lobbied against any Superfund-type legislation in Europe, but they have been dealing with governments—and even opposition parties—not enthusiastic for such laws anyway. The "guidance" of the Bank for International Settlements (BIS), under its Tier 1 capital adequacy requirements, calls on banks to quantify all contingent liabilities. The European banks feel that if they face virtually unlimited and unknowable environmental liabilities, they can hardly quantify contingent liabilities. Since a bank unable to comply with BIS guidelines cannot trade beyond its national borders, such laws could play havoc with global financial markets.

The U.N. Environment Programme (UNEP) recently listed various types of environment-related risks that lenders face now or could face in the near future.[13] These vary in severity depending on the legal regime in place:

• The collateral for a real estate or property to be acquired may be drastically reduced in value if contamination is discovered.

• Borrowers may not repay loans if they have to pay for the cleanup of a contaminated property; fines, penalties, and cleanup costs can weaken the financial performance of a borrower, including undermining the capacity to repay loans.

• In the United States, a mortgage may lose priority to legal requirements that the cleanup takes precedence over loan repayment; some federal bankruptcy proceedings have indicated a priority for cleanup costs over loan repayments, to be paid out of claims against the bankrupt estate.

• The lender might be liable for the extent of any credit extended to any debtor that has operated property containing hazardous wastes, that has generated such wastes, or that has transported wastes in an improper manner; concern remains that potential risks may be extended to all creditors, and not just those creditors holding as collateral property that contains hazardous wastes.

• The creditor may become directly liable for cleanup costs if it forecloses on an owner of contaminated property, becomes involved in the management of the company, or becomes involved in decisions related to the disposal of toxic or hazardous wastes.

• A lender may not be able to pursue its foreclosure options on defaulted loans for fear of liability cleanup costs, thereby having no option but to "walk away" from its loan security.

• A borrower does not maintain collateral or property with an environmental risk potential in an environmentally sound manner, thereby facing direct liability for cleanup costs.

• Aside from statutory liabilities that can be imposed for toxic waste contamination, there is potential liability for personal injuries or property damages, including civil damages.

Initial Responses

Partly as a response to these growing liabilities, some 30 banks, working with UNEP, produced a document entitled "Statement by Banks on the Environment and Sustainable Development" just before the 1992 Earth Summit in Rio. (See appendix for full text.) By mid-1995, 74 banks had signed, with the numbers increasing slowly but steadily. The statement contains a series of pledges, including:

We will endeavour to ensure that our policies and business actions promote sustainable development: meeting the needs of the present without compromising those of the future. . . . We regard sustainable development as a fundamental aspect of sound business management. . . . We are moving towards the integration of environmental considerations into banking operations and business decisions in a manner which enhances sustainable development. . . . We recommend that banks develop and publish a statement of their environmental policy and periodically report on its implementation.

Are the signatories doing these things? Environmental groups charge that they are not. In a certain frame of mind, even the bankers themselves will take pains to explain how difficult it is for them to affect the sustainable development agenda. According to the British Bankers' Association in September 1993: "It is sometimes argued that lenders are in a unique position, or a better position than others, to influence a business's priorities and are therefore well placed to drive forward the higher environmental standards which we all wish to see adopted. This represents a fundamental misunderstanding of the role of lenders and of the depth of involvement in the management of their borrowers' businesses."[14]

But bankers who take this view tend not to be signers of the Statement. At a 1995 meeting, the signatories decided that they needed outside monitoring of their efforts and awarded a contract to do this to an environmental group called Green Alliance.[15] The first study will cover the activities of the 33 banks that signed at the outset in May 1992.

Banks may be pressured by governments to honor their vows—which include recognizing the fact that "environmental risks should be part of the normal checklist of risk assessment and management." In April 1995, Brazilian President Fernando Henrique Cordosa signed a decree making it mandatory for banks and official credit institutions to grant financing only to projects that take environmental impacts into consideration.[16] It gave the Ministries of Economy and Planning and the financing institutions 45 days to establish ways to align their lending and funding with the decree. The Brazilian Federation of Banks later said that it was evaluating the president's "Green Decree."

The differences between the ambitions of the 1992 Statement signers and the view of the British Bankers' Association reflect bankers' struggle to come to terms with rapidly changing attitudes toward the environment, and, more important, to place this pressure in the context of the fluctuating business circumstances in which banks must operate.

It should not be forgotten that the environment is only one of many business pressures that banks have to accommodate while they compete in an increasingly global, deregulated, and technological market. This is why—as with other players in the financial community—the banks' reaction to the environmental question has been to focus almost exclusively on reducing environmental risks in their loan portfolios.

Banks are beginning to take these risks seriously. Some leading institutions have made it clear that they will not lend to companies that ignore environmental risks. This is simply an exercise in minimizing exposure to bad debt. The European banks may be positioning themselves safely in case new laws make banks partly liable for the environmental wrongs of their borrowers.

"We would call this enlightened self-interest, as it is not in our interests to lend to a business which will be unable to repay because of environmental problems," said Hilary Thompson, head of Britain's National Westminster Bank's Environmental Management Unit.[17] "For this reason it makes sense for lenders to integrate environmental issues into their core business rather than increase their own risks. It also makes sense to expect customers to include environmental issues in their own risk management systems. If these are well managed, the business risk decreases, as does the risk to the lender."

The bank has sent a clear message to clients and potential borrowers that they need to reduce their environmental risk or face the prospect of not getting a loan. However, National Westminster also works with customers and potential customers to help them raise their environmental standards.

If banks become too tough on companies in environmental difficulties, they could actually be encouraging environmental damage by denying capital to those businesses, especially small and medium-sized enterprises (SMEs), that need to borrow the capital they require for a cleanup. It is a difficult balance to achieve. This is why banks leading in this field are spending time joining banking and financial-sector business organizations to help develop guidelines and norms.

Banks are grappling with the cost implications of trying to assess risk. This is especially important for the comparatively small loans made to SMEs, the size of which does not allow for extensive (read "costly") risk assessment. The British Bankers' Association points out that the average small business loan is only £20,000 ($31,000), and that "whatever risk assessment of business propositions is undertaken must be cost effective in relation to the amount advanced."[18]

Banks and Small Businesses

The relations between banks and SMEs deserves more discussion in the context of sustainable development. Environmental campaigners tend to focus their attention on big multinational companies quoted on the stock markets, but these are relatively few in number and tend to be improving because of their visibility to regulators, pressure groups, and the public. SMEs, on the other hand, which form the bulk of the world's business community, tend not to be noticed by pressure groups or, unless their pollution is highly visible, the public. And in many developing nations, they are little regulated.

This is true in the developing regions of Africa, Asia, and Latin America. But it is also true in most Northern countries. Some 99 percent of British businesses employ fewer than 50 people, although this figure is elevated because it includes all the self-employed people who have "zero" employees.[19] Most of these small businesses finance a part of their operations by bank credit. Their environmental performance, or lack of it, is having more and more to do with their access to capital, especially to finance the use of clean technology.

In much of the South, the SMEs are equally important to national economies, but their relationships with banks and regulators are often very different than in the North. In Latin America, at least 95 percent of all businesses employ fewer than 50 people, although statistics are unreliable in this sphere, and the percentage is probably even higher.[20]

Most SMEs in Latin America, Asia, and Africa operate in the "informal sector," which means they are outside government and regulatory influence and operate illegally—more outside the law than against it, but often both. They do not do business with legally established banks. In Latin America, SMEs are estimated to provide 35–45 percent of all jobs and account for about 20–25 percent of the continent's economy. Despite their importance to national economies, SMEs are largely ignored by commercial banks in the developing world. There are various reasons for this. Banks there have not faced much competition and tend not to seek new business. Also, as mentioned, smaller loans are relatively more expensive to administer, especially when the borrower operates in parts of the city that bankers are not used to visiting.

As banks in the South learn to do business with SMEs, they have the opportunity to improve businesses' environmental approaches, to improve economic development generally, and to increase their own profitability.

In 1995 the European Commission launched a scheme to help small businesses (typically under 50 employees) gain access to capital for environmental improvements.[21] The businesses obtain the money as bank loans in the normal way, but the Commission acts as guarantor for the loans. The guarantees are given through the European Investment Fund, a partnership formed in 1994 by the European Community, the European Investment Bank, and financial institutions in member-states. The scheme was launched because so many small businesses complained that they could not get money for environmental improvements, even those demanded by law.

Searching for Opportunities

Part of the banks' search for a sensible response to environmental pressures is to find opportunities to make new business and even to create new markets. Opportunities for banks can be divided into internal (making changes in the management and administration of the bank) and external ones (developing new markets and exploiting market opportunities to boost numbers of customers and public image by being seen to be environmentally aware).

One obvious opportunity is for banks to be more eco-efficient in their own business operations by reducing paper consumption, saving energy, and improving transport logistics. Such efficiencies reduce costs and can be used to promote a favorable public image, especially among an environmentally aware and highly desirable market sector: university students and recent graduates.

The Swiss Bank Corporation (SBC) saves about 3 million Swiss Francs ($2.5 million) yearly by optimizing the energy management of their buildings and operations, according to SBC Vice President Franz Knecht.[22] Britain's National Westminster Bank has been particularly active in this area. It surveyed all its facilities and identified various types of environmental waste, mainly in energy, the elimination of which now saves some £12 million ($18.5 million) a year.[23]

In our discussions with bankers, they have pointed to their traditions of a conservative approach to getting into new markets and new "products," or services. They explain this as a reason for their slowness in developing new environment-related products.

The U.S. environmental research organization Worldwatch Institute reports that "traditionally, lenders have treated innovation with scepticism—and higher interest rates—since it increases the perceived risk of a project. But recently a number of banks, often prompted by governments, have realized that by lowering utility [energy] bills, resource-efficient building designs leave owners more money to repay loans, reducing the risk of default."[24] These banks offer cheaper mortgages and home loans for energy-efficient houses.

The Bank of Montreal, for example, offers a quarter of a point off interest rates on loans for houses that fit a certain government energy standard. Sweden also gives cheaper loans for energy-efficient homes, and in the United States, "energy-efficient mortgages" have been available for a decade through some private banks and through federal and state lending agencies. (The international development banks are being pressured to organize the same sorts of programs on a grander scale. Worldwatch argues that, given all the lending for housing projects and buildings that they do, these banks are not fulfilling their development responsibilities if they do not offer financial incentives for energy and resource—mainly water—efficiency.)

Germany's largest bank, Deutsche Bank, has established a European environmental law data base that is available to its customers to help them bring their operations in line with existing laws.[25] Given that small businesses need such a service, the bank sees it as a draw for new customers. The National Westminster Bank has established a computer program called PHAROS that helps customers find out which environmental regulations affect them. They also market a personal computer program that is in essence an environmental auditing package for the Spanish-speaking markets. These are some of the simpler ways in which a bank has turned a potential business liability (that is, their customer's exposure to risk) into a new banking service.

One of the more aggressive marketing campaigns to use the environment was conducted with great success by a previously staid and rather downmarket retail bank in Britain called the Cooperative Bank.[26] It turned its previous losses into profits in 1992/93 by publicizing its ethical stance in an advertising campaign using graphic images of industrial pollution. The bank promised not to lend to companies it deemed to be participating in unethical practices, such as heavy pollution and arms dealing.

As a direct result of the advertising campaign, the Coop's retail deposits increased by 13 percent on a base of 2.3 million customers, with half the new customers mentioning the bank's ethical stance as a reason for joining. Significantly, those attracted by the campaign tended to be wage-earning, responsible, and honest: just the type coveted by retail banks. It has to be said, though, that such a strategy is not open to many banks. The Coop Bank did not stand to lose custom from big business because it had little to start with. A similar campaign by a bigger bank would have affronted some of its most valuable customers. Also, the Coop has been criticized by some environmentalists, and some bankers, for declining to develop and issue an environmental policy and for purchasing goods (chemicals for office machinery and cleaning fluids, for example) from precisely the companies to whom it refused to lend money.

The Sbn Bank, Denmark's seventh largest, has issued what it calls an Ethical Accounting Statement (EAS) each year since 1990.[27] It has little to do with financial accounting, but attempts to "measure the degree to which the company lives up to [the] shared values [of the company and the stakeholders] and thus supplements the statement's bottom line." The EAS is issued along with a brochure explaining the bank's Mission Statement, Code of Values, and the development of their Ethical Accounting. The statement is a direct management review and an analysis of data based on surveys of shareholders, customers, employees, and the community.

Mark Mansley of Delphi International has come up with a list of possible environment-related services banks could offer.[28] In the retail sector, these include selling green/ethical investment products through their retail network, providing loans specifically for domestic energy efficiency, offering more preferential terms on loans for eco-efficient housing, and investigating the possibilities of financing private transport packages other than the traditional car loans. (In most major cities, it is both cheaper and easier to move around through a combination of rented cars, taxis, and public transport, but financial packaging is required to make this truth obvious.)

In the business sector, Mansley notes, possible services include leasing eco-efficient technology, while linking and targeting leasing arrangements to suppliers of such technology; financing corporate energy efficiency; extending work already being done in providing small businesses with information on environmental regulations and on technological solutions to environmental problems; and providing small companies with information on systems to measure and account for environmental costs (and ensuring that lending officers understand and welcome such systems).

Other opportunities include the scope for dedicated sustainable development or environmental banks, such as Ökobank ("Ecobank") in Germany and the Ecology Building Society in England, which lends to environmentally sound projects that might have difficulty getting capital from the traditional market.[29] The South Shore Bank in Chicago helps to rebuild neighborhoods, as does the Community Capital Bank in Brooklyn, New York.[30] Some specialized banks working with the poorest in the developing world, such as the Grameen Bank in Bangladesh, remain not-for-profit.[31] But since this unusual institution began in the seventies, it has made more than 2 million small loans, mostly to women, with a 97-percent repayment rate, and has led the way in showing what reliable borrowers the poorest of the poor can be.

In 1995 the World Bank and nine national donor agencies, which usually deal in grants of millions of dollars, announced they were setting up an organization to finance loans to the world's poor—loans as small as $100.[32] The new organization, called the Consultative Group to Aid the Poor, will be chaired by Bank Vice President Ismail Serageldin, who said when announcing the new Group: "Like slavery in the 19th century, the fact that 700 million human beings are hungry in the 20th Century is unconscionable. We are the new abolitionists."

But this is essentially aid. Some commercial banks are actually beginning to make a business of lending to the poor.

One industrial-country bank to do just this is Bank One of Cleveland, Ohio. Its Chair and Chief Executive Officer Karen Horn explains that her bank was looking for a new market, because, as with most other U.S. banks, its relatively expensive system of branches was being squeezed by other financial services.[33] Cleveland, like most U.S. cities, has a central area with a relatively poor population. Some 60–70 percent of these families have no relationship with any bank, but they do deal with check cashing outlets and pawnbrokers. In 1990, U.S. check cashing outlets earned more than $790 million in fees by cashing 150 million checks worth more than $45 billion, at rates ranging from 3 to 20 percent of the face value of the check. Pawnbrokers, being largely unregulated, can often get away with charging up to 120 percent in interest per year.

"These data told us two things," said Horn. "One, these businesses are quite profitable and, two, they are ripe for competition given the high rates they charge for their services." Surveys found that inner-city families would love to do business with Bank One on the condition that it provided three things: appropriate products, convenient access, and more information. So the bank designed specialized products, set up a chapter in an inner-city cultural institution that people trusted, and provided information relevant to these customers.

"This Community Banking Center now profitably provides customized financial services to a market segment that we—and our industry—had not focused on in the past," concludes Horn. It is also a good example of banks meeting part of the criteria of sustainable development—meeting the needs of the present in ways that benefit the bank and improve the lot of people with serious needs.

Two South African banks, Standard Bank and Nedcor Bank, in 1995 opened new bank chains (E Bank and Peoples Bank, respectively) for poor people who have not previously dealt with financial institutions.[34] The motivation was partly political: the poor are mostly black, and no South African companies now want to be seen to be operating only for whites. But it was also business-oriented, based on hopes that blacks will move into the middle class and maintain bank loyalty.

The poor are expensive customers for banks, in that they maintain small accounts that they access often for deposits and withdrawals. So both banks are relying on the latest automation technology to cut costs. Neither chain issues checkbooks. E Bank clients withdraw money with a plastic card containing a microchip, and the cash card inserted into the automatic teller reads the customer's signature. The bank has been working with IBM to develop a card that carries an image of the customer that cash machines can read. According to Standard Bank, success would make the poor neighborhoods of South Africa the first place where such technology was used commercially. High tech may offer other ways of dealing efficiently, and profitably, with the challenges raised by poor clients.

There are also examples of investment banking that concentrates on environmental projects. The Basel-based private bank Sarasin launched in 1994 a fund called ÖkoSar that invests in shares and bonds of companies with environmentally conscious management.[35] (Other such schemes are discussed in chapter 4.)

Of course, environmental groups will press banks to go even further and to invest in clean energy technologies: "The day the first . . . bank or pension fund invests preferentially in clean energy industries ahead of carbon-fuel industries is surely not far off," writes Jeremy Leggett of Greenpeace.[36] "When that happens, a snowballing effect would seem probable." In the meantime, Leggett advises banks to send market signals by erecting photovoltaic building facades, "which are now cheaper than marble."

Although the environment might still be a concern for only a minority of bankers, there is growing evidence that many are searching for creative ways forward. UNEP helped the bankers draft their 1992 statement on the environment and sustainable development. This U.N. agency continues to work with the bankers, hosting an Advisory Group to the Executive Director on Banks and the Environment, which in 1994 included such institutions as Bank of America, Bank Handlowy, Credit Suisse, Deutsche Bank, the European Bank for Reconstruction and Development, International Finance Corporation, National Westminster, and Royal Bank of Canada.[37]

UNEP organized a two-day roundtable on environmental risk for commercial banks in September 1994.[38] This meeting also served as an indicator of where the banks are in their search for intelligent, business-like ways to deal with environmental issues. Almost every speaker began by saying that the environment was not just about risk but about opportunity. But most speakers then turned to concentrate on risk and liability.

The World Bank and its subsidiary, the International Finance Corporation, are working to develop an environmental impact assessment of businesses and projects that is useful to commercial and investment banks.

Ways Forward

The more progressive bankers with whom we spoke cited several significant steps that every leading bank should take:

• Integrate environmental considerations into core business activities and do not simply add these on as "housekeeping" measures.

• Adopt and practice the principles in the "Statement by Banks on the Environment and Sustainable Development."

• Encourage customers to develop environmental risk management systems as part of broader management systems.

• Participate in the environmental debate, not from a defensive stance, but with the aim of creating new, progressive standards and also new markets with economic, environmental, and social benefits.

We would add, as UNEP suggested in its survey, that national governments and multilaterals have a key role to play in creating "global" guidelines/regulations that would simplify the bankers' approach to crossborder transactions while also setting the stage for a more level playing field.

There is also a clear and significant need for more sophisticated, empirically based risk management tools.

6 The Insurers

The insurance industry is first in line to be affected by climate change. . . . It could bankrupt the industry.

Frank Nutter, President,
Reinsurance Association of America, 1994

The sight of insurance executives mingling with environmentalists and meteorologists at international summits might not be commonplace yet, but it is certainly becoming more prevalent. In 1995, insurers attended a meeting held in conjunction with the Berlin Summit on climate change and designed especially to address their concerns. They were there because they fear that a change in the world's climate—whether as a consequence of global warming or not—might be responsible for some of their recent large losses. Between 1987 and 1993, the world's insurers lost a record $44.2 billion from windstorm damage alone.[1] The cost of massive brush fires in California and Australia in the nineties and unusually bad flooding in Europe in 1995 added to these climate-related losses.

"It would seem that in the face of increased likelihood of extreme climatic events caused by global warming, that it is imperative for insurers to make every effort to mitigate their exposure," concluded a report by the Lloyd's Underwriters Non-Marine Association.[2]

The possibility of climate change, while environmental in nature, creates a set of concerns wholly different from the other environmental problems facing the industry, such as paying for asbestos-related claims and for the cleanup of other hazardous waste in the United States.

Chapter 6 Summary

Environmental claims have been called the insurance industry's black hole, with U.S. insurers facing an estimated $2 trillion in pollution cleanup and asbestos-related claims.

These figures do not include the additional billions that have either been paid or are reserved in the European insurance markets. The problem is so immense that the solvency of this global industry is under threat.

Industrial insurance (as opposed to life insurance) is a $1.41-trillion business—about the same size as the oil industry—with thousands of insurers worldwide. Insurers agree to underwrite the risk of destruction or damage to property, ships, aircraft, and so on in return for fixed payments (premiums) from the insured. The underwriters usually insure themselves—that is, off-load their risk—with reinsurers, a form of wholesale insurance.

Decisions made by insurers are highly influential. First, these individuals have large amounts of cash from premiums, which they invest in the financial markets. Second, in their roles as consultants to the companies they insure, they can influence approaches to environmental management. Third, they can increase business costs by insisting on high premiums for risky activities, and thus they can help change our views on what is risky. And fourth, insurers can and do refuse to insure certain risks, such as gradual pollution.

Even as the industry's solvency is under threat from past environmental liability, another potential danger has emerged: climate change—the theory that human activities are producing a less predictable, more destructive climate. Recent apparent instability in the weather and a succession of natural catastrophes have made it more difficult for insurers to calculate risks.

The insurance industry has begun to respond to these pressures, on both financial and political levels. Examples include the development of financial tools to help business off-load some of its environmental risks, and the drafting by insurers of a U.N. charter on sustainable development. Leading reinsurers such as Munich Re and Swiss Re are taking the idea of global warming far more seriously than others in the business community, and are looking for ways to reduce their risks from unpredictable weather. And in their role as investors, insurers are coming under pressure to redirect their investments into industries whose activities will reduce rather than increase the threat of climate change.

The two sets of problems should not be confused, for the cleanup issues are historical, real, and a direct consequence of legal obligations, while climate change is something that may or may not be happening now and that may or may not become a more serious problem in the future. It is interesting that the insurance industry must cope with two so very different problems: one a historical artifact of the U.S. legal system; the other a present and future global threat.

Concern about climate change (or global warming) is based on the theory that the world is getting warmer as a consequence of the release of several "greenhouse gases," one of the main ones being carbon dioxide, which is building up in the atmosphere primarily due to the burning of fossil fuels such as coal, oil, and gas. These gases trap incoming energy from the sun—the so-called greenhouse effect—a process that could increase average temperatures. This in turn could cause raised sea levels as oceans expand due to warming, and it could add to the overall energy in weather systems, increasing the frequency and ferocity of hurricanes and other storms.

Other theoretical consequences of warming include increases in certain diseases and pests, and more and longer droughts. Some possible impacts are more positive, such as warmer winters (less energy needed in heating), longer growing seasons for crops, and more fresh water, should the warming increase rather than decrease global precipitation.

Industry, which with transport emits most of the greenhouse gases, tends to underplay the issue and call for more research, while environmental campaigners highlight the possible catastrophic consequences of warming and call for government action (such as a carbon tax) to curb emissions.

Weather is what happens locally at a given time, while climate is weather over a region over years or decades. It is difficult to prove that the climate is actually changing from previous averages—of temperature, rainfall, wind speeds, and so on. It would be more difficult to prove the cause of any such change. Yet the Intergovernmental Panel on Climate Change, basing its findings on both computer models and observations, has described itself as "certain" that increases of emissions of greenhouse gases "will enhance the greenhouse effect, resulting in an additional warming of the Earth's surface."[3]

Legacies of Past Decisions

To return to coping with damage from past actions, the estimated bill
for hazardous waste and asbestos damages and remediation in the
United States is $2 trillion, based purely on the projected costs of
meeting U.S. claims against general liability insurance policies written
by U.S. and European insurers.[4]

Asbestos was used widely in products and buildings through the
sixties, before its harmful effects on people's health began to be understood and acknowledged in many areas. Its use in the United States
decreased sharply about 20 years ago, although it continues to be
widely used in other parts of the world and is still imported into the
United States. Companies that were sued for damages by people who
had suffered ill health from the effects of asbestos (or who thought
they might) looked to their liability insurers to pay. Around 200,000
asbestos-related claims have been resolved, but in 1994 a similar number were still pending.[5] It was estimated in 1994 that new claims for
occupational exposure were being filed at a rate of up to 60 a day.

The insurance claims to cover the costs of other forms of hazardous
waste cleanup are mainly, but not entirely, related to the sites where
hazardous waste was dumped in the United States in the decades
following World War II. In the mid-seventies, the U.S. government
ruled that much of this waste had been improperly stored or disposed
of. A 1976 law, the Resource Conservation and Recovery Act, controlled active sites but said nothing about old and abandoned dumps.
Following media revelations about the dangers of contaminated sites,
notably Love Canal in New York State, the Comprehensive Environmental Response, Compensation and Liability Act (also known as
"Superfund") was introduced to clean up abandoned sites. (See chapter 5 for Superfund's effects on the banking community.) This imposed
strict, retroactive, and joint and several liability on those deemed
responsible for the waste (called potentially responsible parties—
PRPs).

"The insurance industry's Superfund nightmare began in 1985 when
a lawyer maintained that his client's General Coverage Liability policy
was in effect at the time waste was dumped and required the insurers
to pay his clean-up costs. The insurers disagreed, and so began a

decade of lawsuits all over the country as other PRPs pursued their cost recovery cases against their insurers," says Mike McGavick, director of the Superfund Improvement Project of the American Insurance Association.[6]

The association estimates that insurers spend about $450 million a year on transaction and legal costs alone for Superfund. Besides Superfund-related claims, insurers are also pursued through the courts to pay for cleanup costs related to gradual pollution by individual companies. Some lawyers specialize in digging out old policies that were written without a time limit for the notification of the claims, known in industrial liability insurance circles as "long-tail," and taking the insurers to court. This practice is often called "insurance archaeology." One well-known practitioner is Randolph Fields, a California attorney and British barrister, who calls himself "a raider of the Lloyd's ark," although insurers would probably choose a less romantic description.[7]

At the time of writing, there were signs that Superfund was being reformed, and Washington appeared in a mood to reduce the number of environmental regulations and ease the impact on business of existing laws. Whatever the outcome, the insurance industry has already suffered heavily and is likely to continue to hurt. At the core of its problem are general liability policies that were written in ignorance of the potential liabilities created by past pollution, or, more important, in ignorance of who society would decide should pay for past mistakes.

The industry no longer writes long-tail policies, and it excludes gradual pollution from environmental impairment cover, which is both costly and difficult to get. But some in the industry feel it should be using its experience with asbestos and hazardous waste to deal with what they see as its forthcoming and rather more complex problem: climate change.

Future Risks

Climate change is a subject on which various industry figures have become quite vocal. In 1993, the president of the Reinsurance Association of America said that the insurance business was the first to be affected by climate change, and that it could "bankrupt" the $1.41-trillion industry.[8] That same year, the world's largest reinsurer, Munich Re, called on governments to take "drastic measures" to address climate change.[9] A second major reinsurer, Swiss Re, warned in 1994 that human activity "could accelerate global climatic change to such an extent that society may no longer be able to adapt quickly enough."[10]

It would be wrong to characterize these and other statements on the subject as the industry shifting toward the environmental campaigners' point of view. But in a sense insurers have a natural affinity with environmentalists. Their business is about both calculating risk and limiting damage so that the amounts claimed against damage and injury are also limited. One way to do this is to make customers aware of safety and prevention practices. So "precautionary behavior" and the precautionary principle championed by the environmental community are natural extensions of core insurance industry practices. Avoiding environmental damage, preventing catastrophe before it occurs, is a goal common to insurers and environmentalists—which is why there is emerging cooperation among insurers, climate scientists, and environmental groups.

Meanwhile, there are clear indications that the ground rules on which insurers have traditionally based their business (using historical data to calculate future risk) are coming under scrutiny. Some influential figures within the industry are questioning the validity of traditional practices and the consequent ability of insurers to remain profitable if the predicted consequences of global warming become a reality.

This sentiment is reflected in the report by the Lloyd's Underwriters Non-Marine Association, which called on insurers to manage their risks better in partnership with customers: "This requires insurers to look forwards rather than backwards in assessing risk, and insurers should actively make recommendations that mitigate risk."[11]

Concern about the possible effects of climate change has been sufficient to lead to a U.N. treaty that obligates signatory governments to reduce their emissions of greenhouse gases, although critics say that the targets are not tight enough. The insurance industry, which of all industrial sectors is first in line to lose out financially from the impacts of warming, has often acknowledged its exposed position.

"We do indeed have a problem [in climate change] and it is far more serious than would appear at first glance," said a Swiss Re report in 1994.[12] In the foreword to the report, Rudolf Kellenberger, a member of Swiss Re's executive board, wrote: "The more quickly and radically the global climate changes, the more extreme weather patterns could cause damage which not only pose a threat to individual citizens, families and enterprises but could also jeopardise whole cities and branches of the economy and—on a global scale—entire states and social systems. In brief: damage which had better not be risked because it can no longer be handled."

This worry is repeated in a 1994 UK insurance report that warns the industry that it "has a limited breathing space in which to gather its wits, and plan in a truly long-term timeframe."[13]

How can the insurance industry plan for a more predictable future in an increasingly unpredictable climate? Some outside the sector argue that climate change offers a great opportunity to insurers. It gives them an ideal excuse to get out of marginally profitable markets and inflate premiums in other markets.

Whatever the merit of this view, the industry is not short of suggestions on how it can use its own influence to help curb the emission of greenhouse gases and thereby help to mitigate its risks. Ideas for action range from the purely practical, such as insisting on better building standards to reduce energy consumption, to the political, such as lobbying for the encouragement of such energy sources as solar or wind.

These ideas, which are worth looking at in greater detail, are largely the work of environmental campaign groups, which are trying to use the problems of the insurance sector to undermine the lobbying power of carbon-fuel producers and their major customers. They also want insurers to encourage reform in the business community by, say, rewarding those who curb energy consumption with lower insurance premiums.

Greenpeace, which has organized a series of well-attended conferences for the insurance industry, wants insurers to acknowledge that their interests are different from those of the carbon-fuel suppliers and users. The group wants insurers to break ranks with manufacturing industry and to lobby government and international forums for policies that penalize the use of carbon fuels and encourage the development of "new and renewable" energy sources: sun, wind, wave, and so on. The campaigners say that this is the only way to reduce the threat of climate change and, consequently, the threat to the profitability of the insurance industry.

The environmental organization lists several activities that it wants insurers in particular, and the financial community in general, to undertake:[14]

• Lobby and contribute to policymaking on climate change. Greenpeace urges the financial community to lobby governments and global forums that devise policy related to climate change. The argument here is that the interests of the financial sector are not being represented in these forums, unlike those of other sectors, such as the oil industry.

• Send market signals about the benefits of clean energy both by investing in it—or in companies selling it—and by using it. Greenpeace wants to promote clean energy, and it wants the financial sector to lead by example and adopt company policies that promote the idea to a wider audience. It argues that these signals (such as building zero emission buildings or cladding offices in solar panels) would not cost any more than traditional alternatives, and would create fringe benefits such as lower energy bills and an improved public image.

• Send market signals by demanding environmental indicators. The financial community should encourage business to include environmental indicators in their financial reporting, Greenpeace maintains. Examples include energy used per dollar of turnover or net profit, or per employee, and carbon dioxide emissions similarly broken down. The group argues that markets should reward those companies with good and improving environmental performances.

Insurers are bemused by these suggestions, especially those on preferential investment. They accuse campaigners of being naive and ignorant of investment practices and the regulatory regimes under which they have to operate. They also point out that the majority of most insurance companies' profits are invested in government bonds, an extraordinarily conservative approach. This is done to protect the funds from erosion so that claims can be paid when they come in. In fact, the European Union issues directives to insurers that limit what can be considered a proper investment.

Some insurers are more receptive to the idea of selective investments, however. They have told us that there are sufficient resources available to create a fund that would be big enough to send a signal to the markets and small enough not to upset the regulators or threaten the prudence of the industry's investment strategies.

The Lloyd's report suggests another strategy, pointing out that the interests of insurers are different from those of the carbon club, but noting that the club has enough power to prevent government from protecting insurers:

It is thus probable that the insurance industry is going to have to take some initiatives either by itself, or along with the banking industry. . . . The insurance industry has over a trillion dollars invested, and even a small shift could send a message which could be important and initiate a gathering momentum. . . . An obvious and perhaps necessary approach is for the industry to sponsor a team to assist in these processes, to monitor and assist developing technologies and to represent the industry's concerns whenever appropriate, for there is little doubt that the influence of insurers and their ultimate benefit is dependent upon a continuous presence being felt.[15]

The suggestion that the insurance industry should present a unified lobby against the carbon club has many difficulties, not least the question of what it should be lobbying for. But there is a more practical problem that is related to the highly diversified nature of the insurance industry. While the oil industry is dominated by a relatively small group of major players, the insurance industry has at least 300. Getting so many players to sing with one voice would require great political skills.

Taking Action

At least one big reinsurance company has gone far beyond defensive thinking to seize the opportunity of making new business out of environmental challenges. Am Re Corporation, with assets of more than $6 billion, is the parent company of American Re-Insurance Company and of Am-Re Services Inc.[16] The latter seeks out innovative young companies developing technology for environmental waste elimination or cleanup. It offers them help in technology transfer, sales and marketing, and technology reviews, and it also offers basic business consulting.

With 27 offices in North and South America, Europe, Asia, Africa, and Australia, Am Re can help companies with their international technology and marketing strategies. It can also advise its insurance clients on how the products of these companies may help them decrease their environmental risks. In return, Am Re takes equity holdings in the young companies.

Am Re, which has taken out ads in the business press saying "We're looking for a few good companies to help clean up the planet," thus gets an early warning as to the up and coming environmental companies, makes a business out of helping them, and helps their clients. It also secures a firm niche in the "enviro-technology" sector, which they believe "will be one of the next high technology growth areas," from $200 billion spent in 1994 in keeping North America clean to an estimated $400 billion in the year 2000.

UNI Storebrand, a Norwegian insurance company that has a 40-percent share of the casualty and property insurance market in Norway and is the largest private-sector institutional investor on the Oslo Stock Exchange, has published and begun implementing its own Environmental Action Plan.[17] This covers such things as over the next three years declining to do business with car repair shops that are not environmentally certified. It also will not provide coverage to ships that do not meet standards for bunker fuel, refrigerants, personal safety, and docking and unloading procedures.

The company planned to launch in late 1995 a $30-million UNI Storebrand Environment Fund, selecting stocks based on a set of sustainable development categories, including such concerns as companies' eco-efficiency, product stewardship, and environmental liabilities and opportunities. The fund was to invest in a range of sectors, including metals, forestry, manufacturing, chemicals, and services, the goal being to gain experience with such a screening process so that this investing could be extended to core portfolios. When UNI Storebrand announced that it would include environmental criteria in investment practices, companies and analysts immediately contacted the insurer to ask what sort of environmental indicators and reporting it would be seeking. This indicates the sort of influence wielded by an insurance company's investment strategy.

The insurance industry has made some progress in working together. The United Nations Environment Programme (UNEP) has been working with it to encourage a better understanding of climate change. UNEP Executive Director Elizabeth Dowdeswell told the Berlin Summit in 1995 that she was encouraged by the interest of the insurance sector: 'Recent statements from the insurance sector are a welcome reminder that there is not a single unified industry position in the climate change debate, opposing all proposals for greater efforts to address the potentially devastating effects of climate change."[18]

Some leading insurers—among them UNI Storebrand of Norway, Swiss Re, Gerling Global Re of Germany, and General Accident of the United Kingdom—are currently preparing a statement on environmentally sound and sustainable development.[19] They planned to have the document, modelled on the bankers' statement on sustainable development, ready for signing in late 1995.

Using Insurance and Finance to Control Risk

On a more practical level, the insurance industry has been developing products that are designed to help industry reduce its potential liabilities from environmental damages. However, in simply consulting and negotiating with potential clients about environment-related insurance, the insurers can help companies improve policies and practices. Part of their influence stems from the fact that insurance companies usually have more practical knowledge of risk than the company seeking insurance. So more and more insurance companies are going into the risk consultancy business.

The new products offered range from traditional policies (very specific and with many exclusions) to hybrids that combine insurance with financial tools. In certain circumstances, some products can be used as a vehicle to finance cleanups.

Insurance companies are becoming more careful in checking potential clients' own efforts to reduce their environmental risks. They require that the companies be able to demonstrate the efficiency of their environmental management systems. But no matter how good their management, companies in inherently risky sectors can only reduce, not eliminate, their risks. Insurers are useful in helping to manage the risk that remains.

There are two types of environmental coverage: pure risk transfer, as typified by third-party pollution liability, and a combination program that uses both self-finance risk management techniques and risk transfer. Risk transfer policies typically cover third-party bodily injury and property damage claims.

Combination programs can be designed to cover both first- and third-party claims through the use of financial techniques that allow the corporation to set aside and use its own funds against a potential risk. These highly flexible programs, which are tailored to the specific needs of a company and will not be described in any detail here, are true hybrids of insurance and structured finance. Either style of coverage—or a combination—can be integrated into an environmental management system.[20]

More specifically, the insurance industry offers five different types of coverage. Each addresses a specific risk—no single product covers all environmental risks. The policies are commonly available in the United States, with similar products on offer internationally.

• *Directors' and officers' coverage* covers losses from claims brought against directors and officers of a company as a result of a pollution incident. This type of policy differs from the others in that it excludes bodily injury and property damages but covers potential losses to the company caused by the way management responded to an incident. It covers all subsidiaries and sites that fall under the authority of the directors and officers; most environmental policies are specific to a particular site.

• *Third-party pollution legal liability,* also called environmental impairment liability cover or pollution legal liability coverage, covers claims made by third parties (such as a neighbor) for bodily injury and damages to property caused by pollution coming from an insured site. Policies also usually cover the third party's bodily injury and property damage, including the insured's legal defense fees.

• *Contractors' pollution liability cover* is similar to environmental impairment liability and covers contractors for claims arising from pollution caused when working on sites belonging to others.

• *Compulsory own-site cleanup* or *environmental remediation insurance* is designed to protect buyers of commercial property from the cost of cleaning up pollution they did not know about. The policy is only issued once the site has been investigated. It covers the possibility that something might have been missed.

• *Professional indemnity coverage,* also known as errors and omissions coverage, is designed for professionals performing environmental services and covers them for claims made against any negligent acts and errors that result in pollution or loss of use.

All these policies are underwritten on what is called "claims-made" rather than the more traditional occurrence policy used for general liability. This is because environmental problems, such as a leaking underground oil tank, can take many years to be discovered. Claims-made policies limit the time period of the insurer's risk.

Ways Forward

The insurance industry, or at least big parts of it, is demonstrating that it is aware of the environmental threats to its future. It is working on a practical level to improve products that help others to reduce their exposure to environmental risk. By developing a statement on the environment and sustainable development, the industry is showing that it understands the need to be politically active on the world stage. It needs to seek other ways of showing its real concern with environmental risks.

Given its painful experience with asbestos and hazardous waste cleanup, it would be surprising if the industry ignored what some of its members see as signs of climate change and thus of increasing property damage. But it is still unclear whether insurers have either the unity or the political will to work together or to encourage others in the financial community to work for structural changes that will reduce the risk of global warming.

It would appear that the very least the industry should do is use its power with its clients to help them understand and protect themselves against environmental risk, through management techniques as well as through insurance. The industry can also organize itself to lobby and influence policy as effectively as some of the other, currently better organized sectors of business and industry.

7 The Accountants

For the first time in accounting's sleepy history, there is a growing recognition among accountants and non-accountants alike that accounting, that value-free, balanced system of double entries, may be sending dangerously incomplete signals to business, to consumers, to regulators, and to bankers.

Daniel Rubenstein, Office of
the Auditor General, Canada, 1994

For a profession that labors under the reputation of being a fountain of boredom, the accountancy business is attracting a surprising amount of interest among environmental campaigners. By far the most prevalent pressure on accountants is the demand from all players in financial markets to put a price on the environmental risks faced by companies. These are the business risks that have an environmental influence and can reduce the value of a company: contaminated land, polluted groundwater, environmentally unsound products, and so on.

The list is growing fast. Increased awareness of the health of our environment has created a new set of risks, some dictated by new laws and others by shifts in the market to accommodate new political and consumer concerns.

Environmental risks faced by a company can be either a regular cost of doing business (such as high waste-disposal charges or gradual loss of market share due to consumer reaction), or a liability (legal requirements to clean up contaminated land, for example), or some combination of the two. They vary according to industrial sectors. Those of, say, the nuclear industry will be different from those in the food sector. There are, however, many risks that are shared by most industrial companies.

Chapter 7 Summary

Accountants and auditors are coming under increasing pressure to include environmental information in the accounts of both companies and countries. The feeling among some, both within and outside the profession, is that the social costs of trade and industry should somehow be reflected in the accounts. Externalities, such as pollution, should be internalized so that the price of a shirt, a cake, or a car reflects its impact on the environment.

The pressures stem from the supposition that accountancy should put a financial value on what society treasures—and it should be quick to follow social trends, such as the interest in sustainable development. These are relatively new and deceptively complex arguments to which the accountancy profession has reacted in three distinct ways.

First, it has adopted a studiously cautious approach befitting its reputation. It has, on the whole, suggested that its role is that of a referee, checking to see that the game is played according to the rules; it is not the maker of rules. Accountants say if the rules are to be changed, well and good, but it is up to others to change them. However, their reaction is not entirely neutral. Accountancy academics have put forward some important suggestions on how the profession could better reflect society's changing values. Although their recommendations have yet to be acted on, professional bodies have produced discussion documents that have tried to accommodate some of the ideas.

Second, accountants and auditors, not averse to making new business, have identified clear opportunities to profit from the pressures by adding environmental services to their portfolios. These range from auditing the environmental performance reports produced by companies to offering advice—in conjunction with technical and legal experts—on the environmental implications of mergers, acquisitions, and takeovers.

Third, the more forward-thinking individuals in this field have acknowledged that the environmental pressures will eventually be reflected in their work (especially in identifying business risks) and are trying to develop the necessary expertise within firms to support and add value to their traditional services.

Meanwhile, the accountancy profession remains firmly in the environmental spotlight, mainly because of its function as an interpreter, verifier, and, to a certain extent, reporter of business information to the markets. It is, after all, the final arbiter on what constitutes the bottom line. Auditors are also being pushed into a corner, as they carry unlimited liability and are a set of deep pockets to whom society could seek redress in the future for any failure to offer the right signals now.

The capital costs of complying with pollution control regulations can be high, but the financial risk associated with contaminated land and groundwater can be much higher, mainly because of the astronomical costs of cleanup and the fall in value of the affected land. Much contamination results from once common industrial practices that, although now known to be environmentally damaging, reflect unawareness rather than malice and demonstrate society's very recent ignorance of the effects of pollution. These include practices such as allowing chemical solvents to seep into the ground; letting lead dust settle in buildings and on the soil; dumping unwanted chemicals, coal tars, and asbestos on site; and so on.

Most industrial sites suffer from some form of contamination, as do many commercial buildings, such as offices and shopping arcades, built on previously contaminated land. But the measurable financial risk of this contamination—the potential liability—differs according to three main factors: the legal necessity to clean up or to declare the liability; the company's own decision on the timing of cleanup; and, if the asset is to be sold, the market's estimation of the contamination's impact on the land's value.

Laws on cleanup and contamination differ quite dramatically between countries and are still being developed. The Netherlands, for example, insists that all land should be restored to standards suitable for agriculture, no matter its intended use.[1] In the United Kingdom, however, the standards are far more relaxed, and the level of cleanup can match the intended use. As a result, cleaning up land to build a car park costs a lot less than for a school or home site, for example.

Most national laws are stricter on pollution of groundwater, especially when it is used as drinking water by the community. In these cases, companies can be forced to pay for the fastest possible purification of underground reserves, a costly process. Whether these costs—or potential costs—appear in the accounts of a company depends largely on the interpretation of the law and the intentions of the particular business. Companies operating in the United States, for example, are required by Securities and Exchange Commission (SEC) regulations to disclose large environmental exposures.[2] This means that U.S. accounts often show provisions that have been made for future cleanup, but it does not necessarily mean that all exposures are disclosed.

A Price Waterhouse survey of 1,100 U.S. companies found that 62 percent of respondents made no mention of their environmental exposures.[3] This demonstrates, according to the firm, that although the companies might privately acknowledge their environmental costs, many decide either through choice or ignorance of regulations not to go public on the matter.

Understanding Market Demands

If the law in most countries is slow to encourage companies to reveal their environmental liabilities, the markets themselves are being more persuasive. And the role of the accounting profession in interpreting market demands and supplying information wanted by markets is growing. This is especially obvious in mergers and acquisitions (M&A), where accountants—as financial advisers—are called on to verify valuations of land assets and capital equipment (which might become obsolete faster than expected when environmental regulations or market demands change).

M&A work by accountants is also putting the spotlight on other environmental issues that might affect the future profitability, and indeed the viability, of businesses. This is particularly significant in manufacturing industries, where on the one hand many traditional processes are coming under stricter legal control (and therefore costing more to run), and on the other hand many products are losing market share because of their detrimental impact on the environment (which makes them more costly for customers to use).

It is worth looking at these issues more closely because they highlight a potential cause for concern: that accountants are being asked to evaluate environmental risk without any clear guidelines on how to do it.

Take the issue of volatile organic compounds (VOCs). Many industries use these substances to remove grease from parts, to thin printing ink, to make paint, to mix pharmaceuticals, and so on. The traditional benefit of VOCs is their ability to "disappear," to evaporate once the page has been printed or be distilled off once the medicines have been mixed. The problem is that the solvents do not disappear. Unless they are caught before going up the chimney, they collect in the atmosphere, react with sunlight, and contribute to the formation of unhealthy urban smog and ground-level ozone.

New legislation in Europe has, broadly speaking, forced manufacturers to capture the VOCs rather than let them evaporate into the atmosphere. This has pushed up process costs because new equipment has been needed to comply with the law. The result has been a shift away from chemical solvents to the use of water. Paints, polishes, and printing inks are among the products that have been reformulated to reduce their VOC content.

Fascinating for technologists, but what is the relevance for accountants? There are two issues here: one concerns simple accounting procedures and the other, valuation.

The profit and loss account can be affected by the increased cost of controlling pollution, higher prices for the disposal of waste, and reduced margins on products that are considered to be less in demand because they are environmentally unsuitable (such as a refrigerator that uses chlorofluorocarbons as a coolant or an asbestos brake-pad). Furthermore, depreciation charges could rise to compensate for the reduced life of plant, equipment, and buildings that cannot be adapted easily to meet new standards.

That is mostly bread-and-butter stuff to accountants, as long as they are aware of these legal, technical, and market changes. Far more interesting, because of its complexity, is measuring and assigning value to companies that are grappling with the environmental pressures on their business. In a straight value comparison between a slow-moving company that still relies on VOCs, either in its processes or its products, and a leading one that does not, it can be argued that the lagger will suffer a penalty and will therefore be worth less than the leader.

What is new here is that these risks have an environmental element to them. But the main principle remains familiar and relevant: does the company have a future in a changing world? The difficulty for accountants and auditors—and this is a problem for all those professionals involved in valuation—is estimating the size of the financial penalty or bonus, and the timing of its impact. In the real world, leaders do not always win, nor do laggers invariably lose. For example, early adopters of new technologies and processes might lose because the markets could take much longer than expected to recognize the benefits. Or a solution introduced later on might simply prove more effective.

Consider the waste management companies that built incinerators in the United States and Europe on the expectation that laws would force industries to burn certain wastes. Not only did the laws fail to materialize in the form expected, but to avoid the high cost of incineration, companies switched to processes that avoided the production of wastes. Another example, this time in the United Kingdom, is the standards applied to landfill. The waste companies that applied the strictest standards to their landfill sites because they believed government promises of enforcement have discovered instead that they are being undercut by competitors working to much lower standards and exploiting government lethargy. The high-standard operators not only suffer the impact of lower revenues, they must also service the cost of borrowing to finance the higher capital expenditure needed to meet the better standards.

Pity the accountant charged with measuring the value of such operations; there are no established rules and few benchmarks on which to base a judgment. No wonder accountants remain hesitant on these matters. Hesitant, perhaps, but not paralyzed. Auditors themselves are suggesting that they should consider giving more weight to the future viability of businesses rather than emphasizing a company's historical record.

This shift in emphasis, if it happens, is very much in the future and currently constitutes little more than ideas in discussion papers, such as one produced by Britain's Auditing Practices Board.[4] It suggests that the financial statement should include comment on the company's principal assumptions and vulnerabilities, along with risks it might face in the future. If these proposals are adopted, environmental issues will most certainly become part of the auditor's concerns.

Internationally, auditors are already debating how they should best reflect environmental issues in their work. A discussion paper by the International Federation of Accountants summarizes the need to accommodate environmental change and suggests ways in which auditing procedures can be adapted.[5] The paper offers guidelines in three areas: planning an audit, detecting indications of material misstatements in the financial statements, and understanding how to use an environmental expert.

The very existence of the paper indicates that auditors are acknowledging that environmental risks are important and that they should be reflected in the statements they audit.

What Is an Environmental Cost?

It is reassuring that the accounting profession is looking at ways to accommodate environmental issues, but there is as yet no clear way forward on setting universally agreed standards.

The International Federation of Accountants, whose objective is to harmonize accounting standards worldwide, has a considerable task in the environmental arena. In the United Kingdom, for example, there are no specific requirements to report on environmental impacts, and there is no formal way to be sure that these issues are properly reflected in the accounts. Yet in the United States, as noted, public companies are required under SEC rules to report on environmental expenditure and provisions. So some European companies—especially those with U.S. holdings—are developing policies on how to cope with environmental liabilities. Generally, the trend is that liabilities enter the accounts only when there is a definite requirement to clean up (a firm decision by management or by force of law) and that the figure stated should be at the low end of possible costs.

Another area of concern for in-house accountants is the level of environmental expenditure that should be revealed, or be labelled as "environmental." This is because some companies are beginning to balk at demands to publish a figure for their environmental expenditure that they say is misleading and sometimes meaningless. There is a genuine concern here: a figure becomes more difficult to formulate—and therefore increasingly meaningless to compare—as companies integrate environmental safeguards into every aspect of their activities.

Lack of comparability is partly due to the absence of any universally agreed standards on what constitutes an environmental expenditure. There are also differences in what a company chooses to reveal—usually to improve its public image—and what it is legally obliged to report, which will differ according to prevailing accounting conventions (national and regional) and the sensitivity of its shareholders.

Developments in accounting standards are discussed later in this chapter, but it is worth looking more closely at how accountants are grappling with the responsibility for controlling environmental costs and communicating the significance of those costs to the markets.

Broadly, environmental expenditure can be divided into four main areas: capital expenditure, operating costs, remediation, and (although this might be disputed by some) research and development (R&D).

• *Capital expenditure:* This will include investment in so-called end-of-pipe treatment: new plant bolted on to the old, specifically designed to reduce or treat wastes, such as flue scrubbers and effluent treatment works. But increasingly companies are rejecting end-of-pipe treatments in favor of clean technology. Cleaner production integrates environmentally sound methods into the design of the equipment and the production process, making it more difficult to isolate the environmental costs of a new plant.

• *Operating costs:* The cost of dealing with wastes (incinerating, landfilling, and so on) in order to stay within the law (that is, compliance costs) is charged against profits. So is the depreciation of the plants that have been installed to deal with wastes. A new plant with clean technology built in will have lower environmental operating costs because its design should drastically reduce the amount of wastes and emissions. Fines for breaking environmental laws and the related cleanup costs could be—but are not necessarily—treated as operating costs.

• *Remediation:* Some of industry's contaminated sites and polluted water sources must be cleaned up immediately to comply with laws. Or, when possible, a company may leave a problem until cost-effective technologies are found to clean it up. But contamination could create a liability, the size of which is determined by factors such as locality, what the law says, and whether the land needs to be sold or transferred—say, in a merger or takeover.

• *Research and development:* Pressure to improve environmental performance has created many opportunities for companies to research, develop, and market products and processes that meet a growing demand for environmentally sound goods. Such R&D costs could be labelled as an environmental expenditure if a company wanted to enlarge its published figure. The reverse would be true if it needed to keep that figure small to appease concerned shareholders.

These different categories make it hard for accountants, as there is considerable overlap, and accounting conventions differ around the world. It is also easy to spot a problem emerging for eco-efficient companies trying to communicate to stakeholders what their accountants are telling them. If environmental costs do become deeply integrated into company accounting systems, and if companies do opt for cleaner technology, then the amount companies are spending on clearly identifiable environmental costs falls steadily. This is good for the company and the planet, but it could require some careful explaining to the public. For the moment, this is a difficulty for only a small number of companies.

To implement an integrated approach to environmental management, a company must first get a better handle on the environmental element of production costs. So a change in the ways in which it accounts for costs is essential. Traditionally, most environmental costs borne by companies have been pooled into general overhead and spread across production processes because such costs as waste disposal and emission control, until recently, were relatively small. But with the steep rise in these costs, the identification of the environmental element of a product's total cost is becoming essential to allow a business to evaluate the profitability of specific products.

A study by the Washington-based research group World Resources Institute shows that environmental costs can be high: more than 22 percent of the operating costs at one of Amoco Oil's refineries; 19 percent of the manufacturing costs of a single chemical additive used by Ciba; and more than 19 percent of the manufacturing cost of one pesticide made by DuPont.[6]

Although the study confirmed the difficulty of defining environmental costs, it also demonstrated that a good understanding of the source and size of environmental costs, however one wants to define them, can help companies assess the viability of certain product lines. Moreover, greater clarity on cost could help shed light on the size of a company's total environmental expenditure. This figure is increasingly being demanded by the markets as an indicator of environmental performance. But there is as yet no standard way in which it is reported, if at all.

U.S. and British companies tend to adopt a policy of reporting only that expenditure on the environment that is incremental and directly linked, while attempting to ensure that full provision is made for future costs of cleanup. But many companies in the rest of Europe identify and report all costs that can be even indirectly linked with the environment. They believe that a large expenditure demonstrates a high degree of commitment. Yet as we suggested earlier, it could also indicate failure.

Clearly, some form of standardization would enable markets to make meaningful comparisons.

Setting Financial Accounting Standards

Many different bodies are working on standards, each from a slightly different starting point and within a different organizational culture. The SEC, the European Union (EU), the U.N. Intergovernmental Working Group of Experts on International Standards of Accounting and Reporting (UNISAR), and the Canadian Institute of Chartered Accountants are all more or less independently discussing the same issues and working on similar guidelines.[7]

Despite these efforts—or perhaps because of the many disjointed efforts—progress has been slow. This, of course, pleases those who adopt the "business as usual" approach and would not welcome new standards. But it is significant that two leading commentators within the accountancy profession, Rob Gray (Matthew Professor of Accounting and Information Systems in the Department of Accountancy and Business Finance at the University of Dundee, Scotland) and Daniel Blake Rubenstein (a chartered accountant and Principal in the Office of the Auditor General in Canada), are calling for fundamental changes and for acceleration of progress toward them.

Says Gray: "Business cannot fully embrace the necessary environmental changes until accounting and finance have done so. For these pragmatic reasons if for no other, accountants must learn to incorporate environmental factors into their more traditional roles."[8]

Says Rubenstein: "For the first time in accounting's sleepy history, there is a growing recognition among accountants and non-accountants alike that accounting, that value-free, balanced system of double entries, may be sending dangerously incomplete signals to business, to consumers, to regulators, and to bankers. The imperative to reconsider 5,000 years of accounting conventions is not a passing fad."[9]

Nevertheless, Rubenstein's is still a minority view. Although some academics are indeed talking about far-reaching changes to accounting theory, the main thrust of what is still a gentle debate within the profession is focused on adapting present practices to accommodate shifts in emphasis, such as better identification of costs and potential liabilities.

The only real worldwide accounting standard-setting organization, the International Accounting Standards Committee (IASC), occasionally has been charged with being on the fringes of international accounting and with producing standards of the lowest common denominator.[10] But because of attempts at harmonization, its work has recently become more important. The SEC has already explicitly accepted some IASC treatments by foreign issuers, and the Tokyo Stock Exchange implicitly has done the same.

A significant agreement in July 1995 between the International Organisation of Securities Commissions and the IASC will help create the basis of a global accounting language.[11] This is much needed because at the moment companies must satisfy each applicable securities body in the country where they wish to list their stocks. This is difficult to do, as it often happens that the accounts prepared in one country cannot be understood by investors or regulators in another. This is one of the reasons why Germany—Europe's largest economy—has only one company, Daimler-Benz, listed in the United States.

By 1999, companies that conform to IASC rules should be allowed to list their shares on capital markets anywhere in the world. These rules still have to be worked out in detail and, at the time of writing, it was unknown what, if any, environmental elements would be present. But given that the United States now makes the greatest environmental demands, and that the IASC rules already comply with those of the SEC, it seems probable that there will be at least a nod toward the environment.

Besides the United States, the only other countries to demand some form of environmental disclosure in companies' financial accounts are Norway and Canada. The Norwegians, who have led the U.N.-sponsored debate on sustainable production and consumption issues, are more active than most in trying to put a price on the environment. But the disclosures demanded by Norwegian law lead only to soft statements about compliance with other laws rather than any concrete financial information.[12] The Canadian Standards Committee has approved an accounting standard on remediation costs developed by the Canadian Institute of Chartered Accountants.[13]

Such developments are encouraging, but the slow progress to date in securing universally agreed standards could create problems down the line. If the work toward harmonizing accounting conventions is not more successful in the near future, the variety of recommendations, guidelines, and standards could multiply, attracting into the fray still more standard-setting boards and accountant associations.

Clearly, such a development would confuse the markets further. The obvious danger is that without standards, the companies that are making progress toward eco-efficiency will find it even more difficult to communicate their success to the markets.

The problems facing standard-setters discussed here have to do with improving financial accounting so that it better reflects the financial successes and failures of companies' environmental management practices. Another related but wholly different issue that we have yet to discuss comes under the heading of "environmental accounting." This involves attempts to create completely new forms of accounting that allow professionals to price and cost a range of environmental resources that have no formal price, such as clean air, a predictable climate, healthy seas, and an intact ozone layer. It would also allow accountants to price and cost a range of environmental services not normally given a value of any sort. For instance, you can buy a forest, but what is the value of that forest in terms of its protection of the plant and animal species it contains?

The supposition is that current accounting practice is too limited to deal with such issues. Daniel Rubenstein lists six limitations:

1. Accounting is restricted to dealing with legislated social costs, such as environmental fines, a company must pay. Traditional accounting

rules do not account for the full costs of production, including natural capital such as air, water, or fertile land because society has not legislated that it should.

2. Traditional accounting rules record the costs of environmental investments in the costs of production, but there is no recognition of their less tangible benefits. Without "putting-it-right" accruals (e.g., accruals to decommission a mine), current application of the rules can penalize rather than encourage the environmentally responsible corporation.

3. Accounting has not yet dealt with the notion of inherent limits to economic activity.

4. Environmental concerns require a long-term view. Accounting's definition of an asset is forward looking, but is it sufficiently forward looking?

5. The traditional accounting entity is the firm. To properly account for air and water, the entity would have to be the firm in the context of the natural capital upon which it is economically dependent but may not own in the conventional sense of private property.

6. And perhaps most important, accountants see both profit and all the thorny equity questions implicit in profit as a return on risk. The critical question is whether going-concern and low-occurrence-high-magnitude risks should be recognized before the traditional residual profit is calculated.[14]

If we worry about these limitations, and believe that the accounting profession should play a large role in setting them right, there are some huge steps to be taken before traditional accounting practices can account more fully for the environment. Clearly, such developments are a long way off and will not affect daily business for some considerable time. Can business therefore breathe easy?

The answer must be no, for public pressure is creating an accelerating pace of change in the way countries account for their natural assets. The latest report to the Club of Rome, *Taking Nature into Account,* which calls for the replacement of the gross national product with an eco-social product, is only the most recent in a long string of arguments for a better system of national accounting.[15] The United States, Norway, and the Netherlands are already making progress, and the

European Union is exploring the potential of including more environmental data in national accounts.[16] The importance of finding acceptable ways to put a price on nature is even more pressing in the developing world, and the United Nations is working with Mexico, Papua New Guinea, and Thailand in seeking ways to integrate economic and environmental accounts.

If country accounts—and indicators such as gross domestic and gross national product—are to become more environmental, then the pressure will fall on business accounts to do likewise. After all, national accounts depend heavily on data collected from the business community.

Stretching the Boundaries

If business is to account for the environmental impact of its activities, today's accounting systems will have to be changed dramatically. "The very framework of conventional accounting will have to be rebuilt from scratch," says Rob Gray.[17] "After all, [it] is hardly a roaring success for conventional business transactions, and to expect it to incorporate environmental and social considerations sensitively—as a long-term prospect—is unwarrantedly optimistic."

But, as Gray also points out, the current system is the only one available. A truly sensitive system would internalize current externalities, such as the health costs of air pollution. But this is clearly very difficult at the moment, mainly because so-called environmental accounting tends to use nonfinancial measures—kilograms and cubic meters rather than dollars and cents.

Still, given that conventional financial accounting is the only available tool, let us see how it is being stretched to include a greater amount of environmental information. The reform of a system, after all, indicates a possible first step toward greater change.

Basic financial accounting apparently does allow U.S. companies to meet their obligations to the SEC of disclosing the costs of complying with environmental laws, including operating costs, remediation expenses, capital expenditure, and contingent liabilities.

But "contingencies" can raise serious problems from both an accounting and an environmental point of view. One of the most active standard-setting bodies dealing with the impact of environmentally induced costs on firms' financial statements is the U.S. Financial Accounting Standards Board (FASB). Its Financial Accounting Standard 5 (FAS5) covers accounting for contingencies, but is it appropriate for dealing with environmental liabilities?[18]

The standard requires recognition and disclosure when it becomes probable that a loss has arisen or a liability incurred. FAS5 is a very broad standard, and there are no specifications to help accountants in the definition of "probable." Imagine a company that for years has legally dumped hazardous waste on a dump site. Then a new regulation is discussed by the lawmakers, one that says that this kind of material should be removed from all landfills and the companies that put it there must pay. Does the company already face a potential liability? When should the costs be recognized? Now? When the law is passed? This scenario is roughly what happened to companies under the U.S. Superfund law, but legal wrangling has meant that years later, many "guilty" companies have paid nothing toward cleanup.

The SEC requires the additional disclosure of liabilities in the Management's Discussion and Analysis (MDA) of any "trend, commitment, event or uncertainty" that is known, cannot be determined to "be not reasonably likely to occur," and is reasonably likely to have "a material effect on the registrant's financial condition."[19] It is difficult to know how to disclose an uncertainty, and which uncertainties to disclose. However, the increasing use of the MDA for environmental reporting is helpful, as it is one of the few forward-looking, as opposed to historical, reporting tools.

Another important question concerning environmental impacts on financial accounting is about measurement. Which financial amount should be recognized in terms of cleanup costs? In most cases, the amounts of future cleanup costs and potential liabilities are almost impossible to assess. According to FASB Interpretation No. 14, if no amount can be said to better reflect the contingent costs, the least costs should be recognized.[20] The EU's draft proposal states that as a minimum, the least costs should be set aside.[21]

Once cleanup costs have been reasonably estimated, how should they be classified? There is no uniformly accepted approach. Are they expenses? Or are they assets, since they presumably enhance the economic value of a property?

The FASB's Emerging Issues Task Force (EITF) first dealt with this problem in relation to asbestos, and this work was then used as a precedent for accounting for other environmental costs.[22] In respect to the costs incurred to remove asbestos, EITF permits capitalization, as long as the costs are incurred within a reasonable time after the acquisition of the property and the asbestos problem was known at the time of the acquisition.

Costs incurred from remediation of contaminated land, however, should be treated as expenses, according to EITF. On the other hand, capitalization is allowed if the costs extend the asset's life, increase its capacity, or improve its efficiency relative to the property's condition when originally constructed or acquired; if they mitigate or prevent future contamination; or if they are incurred to prepare the property for sale. The EU document omits this last qualifier entirely but uses the same wording for the other points.[23] Such inconsistencies in recommendations give managers a large discretionary latitude in deciding how to classify the costs, and they also undermine comparability.

Another problem for accountants is provided by the increased use of "economic instruments"—such as pollution taxes and charges and tradable permits. Take tradable permits, a U.S. phenomenon that may spread. Under such a scheme, each company in an industrial sector receives a permit to emit a certain amount of a particular pollutant. Companies pay a yearly fee for the permit. Companies that do not need the whole permit can sell a portion of the emission rights to a dirtier company that needs more than its original allotment. The idea is that companies can organize their own cleanup in the most effective manner and the most cost-effective time period possible, but dirtier companies are constantly paying more than cleaner companies.

Nobody seems to know how to account for such permits in financial accounting. Are they "inventory" because they are held for sale or consumption? Or are they a marketable security, because they represent a right to a certain form of consumption? Yet they differ from marketable securities in that they might only be partly consumed while the rest is sold.

The way forward is still unclear. Much thought from a wide range of interested parties is needed to bring clarity to the debate and consistency to any practices that might emerge.

What about environmental accounting in the pure sense—the process of putting a price on nature, as discussed in chapter 1 in terms of a new system of national accounts? This type of accounting is far more difficult to grasp because it bears so little relation to financial accounting. In a market, prices and costs can to a great extent be observed rather than estimated. Pricing the environment, however, requires scientific estimation of future costs and guesses as to what society is willing to pay for a certain resource or service not privately owned. One approach involves surveys asking people what they would be willing to pay to visit a given protected area or use a beach. This is often criticized because it does not involve real money.

Obviously, many of the issues that this type of accounting must grapple with are both scientific and controversial. How can you "weight" different toxic pollutants, aggregate different physical units, assess environmental impacts, and consolidate the same emissions from plants in different geographical areas? And to what extent is all this the job of financial accountants?

A few, very few, companies are experimenting in the compilation of accounts that reflect more fully the environmental impacts of their business. Some notable attempts have come from Europe. In the Netherlands, a software company called BSO/Origin has attempted to put a price on most of their environmental impacts.[24] And Danish Steel has published what it calls a "mass balance" of its activities—more traditionally called a PIOR Statement (Pollutants Input-Output Reconciliation).[25]

Although both sets of "accounts" are useless to most players in capital markets, they are a brave attempt to drive the pace of change in environmental accounting and disclosure.

Another helpful concept from financial accounting is "prudence." This implies that preparers of financial statements have to contend with the inevitable uncertainties of life. Prudence requires using a degree of caution in the estimates required under conditions of uncertainty such that expected income is not overstated nor expenses understated.

This comes very close to the "precautionary principle" adopted in theory by most governments. This says that if there is a danger of causing serious or irreversible damage to the environment, policymakers should err on the side of caution in taking decisions. This could mean that in their environmental accounting, companies should not understate environmental liabilities and costs, nor overstate environmental achievements and assets.

Progress in this field will depend on the strength of political demands (led by public opinion) and the response from the accounting profession. Auditors, who have to take a broader view of companies and their viability, could play an important role in encouraging standardization.

What Is Environmental Management?

Environmental management systems, now ubiquitous in large companies, could increase the pressure on accountants simply because the systems are beginning to generate the sort of data that will change management's view of the business, and will therefore have to be reflected in the accounts.

Most big companies, and even some smaller ones, now have someone in charge of environmental affairs. Some companies, especially those in chemicals, heavy industry, and oil, have teams of people managing the environment. Their tasks range from technical to political, advising corporate directors on how to interpret political change and communicate difficult news such as spills and accidental emissions.

Environmental management is an emerging discipline and fast becoming a profession in its own right, with institutes bestowing qualifications and credentials. This was inevitable, given the environmental pressures on business, both legal and market.

These environmental managers possess vast amounts of data on a business, some of which is of great interest to outsiders and therefore to accountants and auditors too. The information ranges from the quantity and quality of emissions to the amount of energy used and the level of compliance with environmental laws. The data are of course also valuable to the company itself, because they help senior management make better-informed decisions.

At one time, the mere fact that a company had a structured environmental management system that carried out the corporate environmental policy and provided information to top management was enough to satisfy outsiders of a company's environmental soundness. But now the public wants more. So environmental managers have been charged with two related communication activities: conforming to independent environmental standards and reporting publicly on environmental performance.

It is somewhat ironic that the United Kingdom, which has a patchy environmental record and has been, perhaps unfairly, branded "the dirty man of Europe," should be the first country in the world to develop a specific and independently verifiable standard on what constitutes good environmental management. This goes under the name of BS7750.[26] Some companies have gained accreditation under this standard and others are likely to follow. There is considerable debate, some quite negative, about the effect the standard will have on the actual quality of environmental management. Many fear that companies will work to earn the "badge" and then cease all eco-efficiency improvement and innovation.

But more relevant to this discussion is the way the market responds to companies who gain a badge of merit. The markets have shown that they approve highly of the British quality standard (BS5750) and the equivalent from the International Standards Organisation (ISO): ISO 9000. (Note that these are quality standards and not environmental ones.) Suppliers have found it easier to convince potential customers of their soundness if they have the badge. Firms dealing with governments also find that things go more smoothly if they can produce a standards certification.

The ISO at the time of writing was launching an environmental standard similar in style to BS7750, to be known as ISO 14000.[27] The European Standards Body was set to adopt the ISO standard, and it appeared likely that international businesses will find it useful as a way of communicating with global markets.

Although accountants might also find conformance with standards reassuring, they are more interested in the relatively new phenomenon of environmental reporting. This is when a company, borrowing heavily from the language of financial reporting, publishes a report on its environmental performance. This is a minority and purely voluntary activity; just a few hundred companies do it worldwide.[28] So standards are only beginning to emerge, and the contents of reports differ widely in both quality and quantity of information.

A typical report will contain statements on environmental policy and, possibly, targets for improving performance. It will then report on achievements against the targets and also supply concrete figures on emissions of various types.

With a few notable exceptions, most reports are essentially technical in nature rather than financial. Nevertheless, accountants are very interested in these reports for two reasons. First, they can provide at least a hint of the gravity of the environmental pressures the company is under, which is very useful in M&A work. Second, and far more important, accountants see business opportunities, essentially in helping companies produce the reports. Auditing firms have begun to provide a statement attesting to the rigor of the system used by the company to collect the published data.

Although the business community has encouraged environmental reporting in principle, the practice is very much confined to specific sectors in which the need to project a better environmental image is critical, such as energy, chemicals, and transport. Much depends on whether governments make reporting mandatory (which looks unlikely) and whether the financial markets begin to take a closer interest in the environmental health of companies. There is a feeling that in the future, companies are more likely to include environmental data in their annual reports rather than produce separate environmental reports. This would actually be a sign that such data are considered more an integral part of the company's recordkeeping and reporting.

At present, all environmental reporting schemes are voluntary. The European Union's Eco-Management and Audit Scheme (EMAS) is an example of a bottom-up, plant-by-plant certification system.[29] It is both a standard for environmental management and a system of plant audits to confirm if the plant is up to measure. Many environmentalists hope that it will be made compulsory eventually. But the EU has yet to encourage the big industries at which EMAS is aimed to adopt the system. Nor are there enough certified auditors available.

The European Commission has asked the Accounting Advisory Forum of the EU to develop an opinion on how to improve reporting on the environment in the annual accounts and reports.[30] These efforts of the EU are related to the Fifth Action Programme on the Environment—"Towards Sustainability"—which also contains an initiative in the area of accounting. The draft covers mainly issues such as recognition of provisions for environmental liabilities and risks, capitalization of environmental expenditures, offsetting of provisions and expected recoveries, and some disclosures.

Complementing EMAS are pressures for a top-down, total corporate account. The Finance Sector Working Group of the U.K. Advisory Committee on Business and the Environment (ACBE), which was set up by the U.K. government to advise it on business and environment affairs, found that the level of corporate environmental disclosure is low, with no standard for the quality of reporting and varying quality of disclosure.[31]

Although regular environmental performance reports are not mandatory in that country, there is pressure from some in the financial and business community to make them so. The ACBE Finance Group said that although "practice in this area is developing fast, the Group is very clear that it wishes to see all companies publishing environmental reports. Action is now required to achieve this." The Group added that "some standards will be required and verification may be appropriate; legislation may also be necessary." And it recommended that the London Stock Exchange consider adopting standards of environmental disclosure as one of the requirements of its listing particulars.

The SEC rulings on environmental disclosure in the United States have already been noted, as have similar but less stringent initiatives in Norway and Canada. The SEC has also stepped up its review of the adequacy of environmental disclosure requirements, using Environmental Protection Agency (EPA) information on companies and EPA staff to train its own staff for environmental liability disclosure review. This development prompted the managing director of British Petroleum, Rodney Chase, to say: "If your experience as a multi-listed, multinational is that SEC lawyers and EPA experts are getting into bed with one another over your case, then you'd better start making an attempt to get your environmental act together, and quickly."[32]

In Japan, perhaps because calls for environmental accountability are not as great as they are in Europe and North America, environmental reporting is rare. Some companies, notably the electricity sector, have reported, mainly in response to a circular on environmental management issued in 1992 by the Japanese Ministry of Trade and Industry.[33]

According to Katsuhiko Kokubu, Associate Professor of Accounting at Osaka City University, and his colleagues, environmental reporting is and will be tightly linked to government initiatives.[34]

Ways Forward

The accountancy profession has made a great deal of progress in thinking about the consequences of striving for sustainable development. It may not have gone as fast and as far as environmentalists want, but some (especially those in M&A work) are further ahead in their thinking than others in the financial community. What remains to be seen is how the practitioners will respond to pressure to change the rules so that environmental risks are better reflected in the accounts.

Much will depend on the information made available to accountants by their clients. The majority of companies simply do not collect the necessary environmental data to give accountants the information environmentalists think they need, nor is the information that is collected presented in a way that accountants can use. But when companies do improve performance in this sector, accountants will have to take notice and change some of the accounting rules, if only to avoid being sued for negligence.

The companies that now strive to improve their eco-efficiency—and therefore possess the necessary environmental information—can only hope that accountants will be better equipped to help them communicate their progress to the markets. This communication is one of the first steps on a long road toward sustainable development.

8   The Raters

The attraction of an environmental risk rating is that it measures, not the "greenness" of a company, but the likelihood that it might lose money for environment-related reasons.

Andrew Hilton, Director,
Centre for the Study
of Financial Innovation, 1995

A traditional company or country rating, such as one from Moody's, indicates the likelihood that interest and debt will be paid on time. Venezuela, with a rating of Ba2, has a lower rating than Japan (Aaa), which means Venezuela has to pay approximately 3 percent higher interest rates on certain bonds.[1]

Ratings are an important tool in the fixed income securities business, and they affect financing costs. But to assign a credit rating to a company is an expensive and time-consuming task. The issuer of a security is charged between $20,000 and $100,000 by the rating agency, and the process takes about four weeks. Ratings have to be monitored and periodically adjusted.

It is important to differentiate between ratings that reflect a company's environmental soundness for the sake of the environment and those that do so for the sake of investors and others interested in the company's financial soundness. This distinction can lead to some confusion over the term "environmental rating." Such ratings were initially developed by individuals running "green investment funds" and focused on what companies were doing to or for the environment. They served the purposes of such funds but were of little use to the financial markets because they did not necessarily reflect financial risk.

Chapter 8 Summary

Give us a simple way to understand environmental information and we will act on it, says the financial community. Various organizations and groups are answering the plea by trying to develop environmental rating systems that mean something to financial markets.

Early rating systems—developed by environmental campaigners of one sort or another—attempted to show a company's impact on the environment. This information, such as the quantity and types of emissions, is useful to ethical investors and environmental activists, but it means little to the majority of the financial community, who are primarily interested in profitability and thus need a rating system that identifies risk.

Investors and lenders want a rating that, as a starting point, tells them whether the company can afford its environmental liabilities, current and future. They also need some insight into the company's abilities to manage and pay for possible future liabilities that may occur from, say, changes in the law or shifts in market demands.

Equally, they would benefit from a rating that includes the upside—the opportunities that would accrue from possible future change, such as the benefits to the nuclear industry if a carbon tax were imposed. Such ratings would be further improved if they included the possible financial impacts of nonfinancial issues created by political interests, emotions, and consumer perceptions.

Providing a simple rating to satisfy these needs has proved more difficult than expected, but there is progress. Two models—neither perfect—have emerged so far. One looks in great depth at a single company, involves site visits and considerable research, and costs a lot. The other is desk-based, provides a rating for a broad sweep of companies, and is cheap to buy.

The financial community has yet to decide whether they want, or indeed need, any form of environmental ratings.

Today a new type of environmental rating is being developed for the financial markets; it relates a company's environmental soundness to financial risk and opportunity. For example, a company may be releasing a great deal of waste into a river. If this is legal and the firm actually has a well-organized system of environmental management, then it might get a low environmental risk rating (a low risk means a favorable rating) by the more recent rating models. It might still get an unfavorable rating from the green funds.

We would argue that this is a temporary dichotomy. As environmental performance comes more and more to be equated with financial performance—due to changes in consumer preferences, regulations, taxes, and so on—then such a distinction will disappear. Indeed, we expect that eventually there will be no need for environmental ratings, as this concern will be covered in standard credit ratings. It will have to be, because an environmental risk will equal a credit risk.

But the focus of this chapter is rating systems that do and could mean something to the markets at present.[2] A number of competing systems aimed at the financial community are emerging; their success depends on whether the markets find them useful or not.

First, it is worth taking a look at the workings of the more traditional credit rating systems. Those who offer these services argue that they already take adequate account of "environmental" effects upon a company's creditworthiness. Environmental risk "is already incorporated within the general risk element at the corporate level," argues Richard Fletcher, a vice-president of Moody's Investors Service. "We've always had the position that our ratings do incorporate impending changes in the scenario, including foreseeable future environmental risks."[3]

People developing new systems obviously believe that they do not.

How Traditional Credit Ratings Work

The purpose of a rating, such as one from Moody's, is to provide investors with a simple system to indicate the relative investment qualities of various fixed income securities. The rating reflects Moody's opinion of the willingness, ability, and legal obligation of an issuer to service the obligations in question in accordance with its terms. The rating agency does not seek to give investment advice or to predict the market risk that may be inherent in a given security. It merely assesses credit risk.

The rating agency, to reach its conclusion, must evaluate the various risks that an issuer faces in its operations. These risks include the political and macroeconomics environment in which the company operates (including regulatory matters), the competitive situation within its industrial sector, its financial structure, and the strategic direction of the issuer's management.

All these factors are synthesized into a symbol: Aaa, Aa1, and so on. The rating agency's key challenge is to have consistency in its ratings across industry lines. Therefore, an A2 long-term rating must reflect the same degree of credit risk (risk of default) regardless of whether the organization being rated is a manufacturer, bank, retailer, or utility. The ratings are meant to be a predictive indicator of credit quality and not simply a report card on past performance. Therefore, any area of risk that could inhibit the ability of the issuer of a bond to service its debt must be included in the rating committee's deliberations and reflected in the rating.

Among the risks evaluated are those broadly defined as environmental, such as any associated with cleaning up ground or water contamination, avoiding future cleanup costs, adhering to regulatory requirements, and so on. Both the company doing the cleanup—whether voluntarily or forced by regulation—and the rater judging the firm's creditworthiness must consider the issue of return on capital expended. Is the cleanup nothing but cost, or is it in the nature of an investment? (See also chapter 7.)

If the effort is voluntary, then a company will normally only make such an expenditure if it meets some minimum hurdle rate, such as the company's cost of capital, and the reasons for investing would be to increase capacity or lower the cost structure. Spending on the environment to stay inside the law could either increase or decrease costs, and an assessment of the impact has to be made by the rater.

At the heart of the assessment is an analysis of the costs and benefits the expenditure might bring. There are normally two types of costs: existing and future. Often environmental expenditure is designed to reduce or avoid future costs, usually brought about by changes in the law.

The analysis must also include any increase in operating costs that may result from changes in the way a company operates. For example, a utility may be forced to switch fuel sources to comply with emissions standards, while also incurring a continuing cost for emissions monitoring. While the impact on future costs of current actions (or inaction) may be less precise than a financial analyst would like, ignoring the potential range of costs is risky. Raters should be including this risk and quantifying it. Decisions taken could have a critical impact on the company's ability to compete and therefore on its financial strength in the future.

Such assessments are necessarily complex because business has to satisfy the differing demands of its constituencies or stakeholders, including shareholders, creditors, employees, and the communities in which it operates. Sometimes the interests of stakeholders might be diametrically opposed: improving local air emissions could satisfy the demands of the neighbors, but if the cost affected profitability, the shareholders might be upset. Raters need to weigh the various implications of environmental risks and actions when making their assessments.

The law remains a key factor in the assessment. Companies subject to significant current or potential environmental costs due to regulations will need to have this risk reflected in their rating. Often these costs may be realized in the future in an amount that cannot be determined easily today.

Oddly, cleanup in one sector may pose risks to creditworthiness for companies in other sectors. In North America, as noted in chapter 7, waste processing companies made certain assumptions based on the amount of waste being churned out. But the production companies took steps to minimize their waste, leading to poor financial results among the processors.

The location of companies and the regulatory environment in which they operate must be included in the assessment. Different economies have different attitudes to the environment: less industrialized countries have tended to be more accepting of environmental impact if it delivers rapid economic growth.

This has led to an uneven playing field for certain products, particularly commodities, that are produced at competitive quality levels under differing environmental constraints. For example, Russia has been a significant producer of both aluminum and nickel over the years, with most of its production for domestic, defense-oriented markets. With the decline in demand from the state, Russia has flooded the West with products priced at or below the cost of production of Western competitors from mills that did not bear the same substantial environmental costs.[4] This led to a dramatic decline in global alumi-num prices, which have only recovered as global production levels, including those of Russian mills, have declined. But the Russian pro-duction process has not been fundamentally changed. This is a nega-tive factor in assessing the credit quality of Western aluminum producers, but can it be called an "environmental risk"?

The number of credit rating agencies in emerging markets has been growing steadily over the past few years, according to a *Financial Times* newsletter about such agencies and their work. In late 1994, it listed more than 3,000 ratings assigned to emerging-market debt issues by 10 international and 20 local rating agencies.[5] According to newsletter editor Peter Elstob, "Regulators of emerging markets view credit rat-ings as an effective way of tackling problems of transparency in their jurisdictions. Investors have already taken on board political or coun-try risks but this is the first time they have had access to local percep-tions of the borrowers' credit risk." A number of the larger international rating agencies, including Standard & Poor's, Duff and Phelps, and IBCA, have been providing technical help to the newer, local agencies.

The traditional raters argue that the process of assessing a rating already takes into account all the environmental factors discussed above. But their critics say that these factors are not, in fact, system-atically considered, mainly because the traditional raters do not fully understand environmental risks, and their methodologies are not geared to quantify them.

The critics' case was bolstered by a survey of the financial industry, mainly banks, sponsored by the U.N. Environment Programme and Salomon Brothers.[6] The report showed that there was a need for analytical data and for risk-quantification tools that were "more meaningful."

A Detailed Environmental Rating for One Company

The alleged inadequacy of existing rating systems has led to initiatives to design ratings that more fully describe the environmental risks for the markets.

It might at first seem strange that existing raters have not exploited what appears to be an obvious opportunity to sell a specialized service to the financial community. But as we learned in looking at analysts and the investment community in general (chapter 4), there is not yet a great demand in this part of the financial community for such a tool. Companies with a good record of environmental compliance have not earned a significant premium in the credit and equity markets, nor have all those with poor records necessarily been penalized (though many have). The softness of commodity prices has also led those in the financial markets to doubt some of the more strident environmental campaigners' claims that the world is running out of topsoil, water, and food.

But another reason may be that the financial markets are confused about the meaning of "environmental risk" and uncertain how to measure its impact. Their experience is limited to large and costly shocks, such as oil spills or pollution lawsuits, and to keeping track of the fast-growing body of law and regulation. They do not know how to judge the environmental risks that a company faces on a day-to-day, non-crisis basis.

This is why in 1995 the U.K.-based Centre for the Study of Financial Innovation (CSFI) published an environmental risk rating of Scottish Nuclear, a then state-owned nuclear electricity generator with two reactors in Scotland.[7]

The utility agreed to act as guinea pig to test whether a rating scheme could be devised that could communicate to the financial markets a measure not of a company's "greenness" but of the effects of environmental pressures on creditworthiness. The scheme concentrated exclusively on the downside. The intention was to create a yardstick with which to measure any company's environmental risk, enabling the market to assess the company's environment-based credit liabilities.

The rating is based on facts and informed judgments about a company's environmental performance. It identified two groups of questions: one largely drawn from observable company indicators and the other based more on opinion. In the first category, five main sets of questions were asked:

• *Regulation:* Is the company in compliance with regulations? Can it afford to comply with foreseeable future regulatory requirements? What would be the costs of failure to comply?

• *Finance:* Has the company made adequate provision for environmental liabilities? Is it insured? Is it able to pass environmental costs on to its customers or must it absorb them itself?

• *Legal actions:* Has it been involved in environmental lawsuits? Are any threatened? If so, what might be the outcome?

• *Management:* Does the company have an environmental policy? Is it adequately implemented and enforced? Does the company conduct an environmental audit? If so, has it acted on its findings?

• *Reputation:* Does the company have a good or bad environmental reputation? Have its products ever been boycotted? Does the company care about its environmental image?

The rating also attempted to assess less tangible indicators in three different areas:

• *Quality of management:* Is management adequately aware of its environmental vulnerabilities? Has it anticipated problems and trained staff to deal with them?

• *Strength of environmental policy:* Is this policy robust? Does it ensure that environmental matters are adequately taken into account in decision-making?

• *Operating environment:* How well does the company get on with its regulators? Is there a high level of regulatory and legal uncertainty? Is the sector frequently subject to public or political controversy?

Once these questions were answered, two other major but more speculative questions were asked:

• How large are the company's potential environment-related liabilities and costs?

• How well placed is it managerially and financially to deal with them?

In Scottish Nuclear's case, the risk rating panel identified 11 categories of environmental risk: regulation, safety/environment, decommissioning, radioactive waste, provisioning policy, legal, suppliers, external pressures, management, business prospects, and financial conditions.

The company was given an A rating, on a seven-point scale, with AAA the best (lowest risk) and C the worst (highest risk). An A is third from the best. Scottish Nuclear was deemed to be "a company with large but well-identified environmental liabilities, and sufficient financial and management strength to absorb all but exceptional risks." It was also thought "able to finance any currently proposed regulatory requirements." Many environmentalists were surprised that any nuclear operation could have received such a favorable rating.

The raters emphasize the experimental nature of the exercise and acknowledge that there is still work to be done in perfecting such a system. But CSFI argues that such a yardstick will enable three things to happen. First, the market will learn to differentiate levels of environmental risk and price them accordingly—something the existing analytical and rating functions have difficulty doing. Second, the development of pricing will pave the way for a new market in environmental risk instruments that could be used as hedges by investors, lenders, and insurers. Third, it will restore liquidity to markets that have seized up through fear of environmental loss.

Such a rating service—which could be provided either by existing credit rating agencies or by a new company—would be paid for by companies wishing to obtain a rating, or by a cooperative of institutional investors. An environmental risk rating could be published separately or as a subset to an existing credit rating. CSFI predicts that as the market's awareness of the environment evolves, environmental risk ratings will lose their importance and their findings will eventually be absorbed into the established credit ratings.

The panel that CSFI put together to produce the Scottish Nuclear rating concluded:

It will be up to the financial markets to judge how useful an environmental risk rating is in financial decision-making. We believe it highlights an important aspect of a company, and one which is increasingly sensitive to the outside pressures of regulation and public opinion—in other words, forces which are to some extent beyond management control. It also touches on some of the longer-term aspects of a company's performance, which should help counter the tendency towards short-termism which is so often decried in today's markets.

Other Rating Systems

CSFI's experiment has not led directly to a commercial product. But some members of its risk-rating panel have been involved in commer-

cial initiatives to sell ratings to the financial markets. These projects—
there were at least four in the summer of 1995—either conform to the
CSFI model (detailed, single-company analysis) or take a low-cost,
broad-sweep approach.

One of the first of the broad-sweep approaches to be launched was
System Based Environmental Risk Rating (SYBERR), developed jointly
by Risk & Opportunity Intelligence (ROI) and Environmental Auditors
Ltd in Britain.[8] SYBERR contains credit risk ratings and environmental
risk ratings on more than 330,000 UK businesses. Additional information and other financial performance measurements have been included to allow for depth and breadth of analysis.

ROI's analysis can be used to create images of the concentrations
and trends in environmental risk. The raters claim many applications
for their system. It can be used to give a view of a bank's portfolio in
terms of its balance of environmental as well as credit risk; to quantify
the environmental risk within a given investment fund, and also identify stocks in which to invest; and to evaluate and prioritize insurers'
client bases according to the extent of potential liabilities.

The Ecco-Check Index, another broadbrush approach, was launched
in mid-1995 and planned to assess 850,000 companies within the first
two years of its operation.[9] The information is available online and
measures both environmental risk and performance. The rating is
aimed at the financial institutions and large companies that might
want environmental performance information relating to their
suppliers.

Among the more detailed approaches, Environmental Risk Management Rating (ERMR) is a British system produced jointly by Grayshott
Corporate Finance and Lloyd's Register.[10] This service, which was still
being developed at the time of writing, is expected to provide a highly
detailed analysis of companies. The wide geographic spread and technical expertise of Lloyd's Register should enable ERMR to rate multinationals, but the cost would be high—up to £30,000 ($46,000) per
rating.

Triumvirate Rating System, another detailed UK initiative, is aimed
primarily at lending institutions.[11] The system is designed to identify,
measure, and model the nature, extent, and significance of environmental risks on loan portfolios.

Strengths and Limitations of New Systems

It is far too early to judge whether these new systems will be accepted by the markets. Both the detailed and the broad-sweep approaches offer benefits, and both have their obvious limitations—price and effectiveness among them. Their acceptability depends entirely on satisfying users' needs.

The main strength of both approaches is the focus on putting a price on environmental risk. Both also avoid any ethical overtones. This may be seen as a strength. But there are situations in which it may be a weakness; it could fail to detect an issue that could cause a political or consumer backlash that would affect a company's credit rating.

One surprising result of the new, "market-friendly" rating efforts is that the "more environmentally risky companies seem to have the lower credit risk," notes David Lascelles, who is both a financial journalist and a chairman of the Advisory Council of the Centre for the Study of Financial Innovation.[12] "This is the opposite of what might have been expected, namely that dirty companies are also the more risky economically." He argues that the reason for this "paradox" is that environmental risk often rises as a company ages and grows. Successful companies also get richer as they get bigger and older. Thus some big, old successful companies in sectors such as chemicals or petroleum may be having major effects on the environment, but their credit rating remains high if they act within the law and are known to have the financial resources to cope with any environmental liabilities that may arise.

It is this contradiction that, for some, identifies a weakness of the new breed of rating systems that concentrate only on environmental risk in the most narrow, financial way. How, they ask, can a big polluter be given a good ranking?

That is why ethical investors prefer ratings that take a broader view. Ökom Environmental Rating System, launched in 1994 by Öko Invest in Germany, has been rating one international joint-stock company a month.[13] The information—targeted at ethical investors—is published in the Öko Invest newsletter and the German financial magazine, *Börse Online*. The Investor Responsibility Research Center in Washington, D.C., provides investor research for more than 500 institutions and large companies.[14] As part of this work it produces two indexes—one on toxic emissions and the other on compliance with the environmental laws. As noted in chapter 3, the group uses these ratings to test for correlation between environmental performance and financial performance.

Other research organizations that offer some form of rating include Centre Info Suisse (analyses of quoted companies), Ethical Investment Research Service in the United Kingdom (ratings of all companies in the *Financial Times* index), Eco-Rating International in Switzerland (ratings of companies according to the sustainability of their operations), and the Council on Economic Priorities in the United States (profiles of companies).[15]

Rating systems aimed at the ethical investment community are clearly targeted, and their audience has a definite need for such research. Traditional members of the financial community have rarely, as yet, expressed a need for environmental information, certainly not in the detail that is now on offer. The new "ethically blind" environmental rating services appear to have been developed in the belief that traditional players in the market should be looking at environmental performance, and that once they realize this, they will buy the services. This is definitely a case of product push, rather than market pull.

Ways Forward

If new rating systems that incorporate environmental risk prosper, it will be because the market players themselves begin to feel the need for the information and demand it from companies, creating pressure on companies to pay for environmental ratings.

Such ratings are an ideal opportunity for eco-efficient companies to broadcast their performance to the markets—assuming, of course, that the markets want to hear about it.

Whatever the future of the upstart environmental rating agencies, and however successful they are at making business, it is highly probable that traditional rating agencies such as Moody's and Standard & Poor's will now make even greater efforts to include environmental risk—and maybe even opportunity—in their ratings.

III The Scorecard

In chapter 1 we introduced seven assumptions that caused us to worry about whether financial markets were supporting the goal of sustainable development, or even the less comprehensive goal of eco-efficiency in business.

Having examined the activities of the various market players, we return to these concerns to see which are justified, to what extent, and what can be done to improve things.

• Sustainable development requires investments with long payback. Financial markets seek short-term payback.

The verdict here must be "case not proved," or "sometimes yes, sometimes no." One study of alleged short-termism in business concluded that "the argument that industrial performance is impeded by the short-term proclivities of financial institutions has the attraction of an alibi for faults nearer home."[1] But it added that even if perceptions differed from reality, even if the financial markets did not promote short-term thinking, the belief that they did could affect business behavior.

Paul Marsh, in "Short-termism on Trial," maintained that U.S. and British companies are too likely to produce numbers that discourage them from embarking on projects with paybacks over the long term.[2] They may set too short a payback period or too high a discount rate. Writing in 1990, he praised Japanese firms for creating a corporate culture that supports long-term projects. But he also blamed business and not the financial markets for the perception that a long-term view is a dangerous luxury.

Other commentators blame the present muddled state of business ownership for the perceived short-term view. If big corporations are owned by institutional investors who exercise none of the responsibilities or ambitions of "real" human owners, and who are themselves subject to measures of their quarterly performance, then these corporations will be judged and will tend to judge themselves quarter-by-quarter rather than over years.

We have acknowledged that there must always be a dynamic tension between short- and long-term planning, as without a relatively successful short term, there can be no long term, successful or otherwise.

Yet we are also convinced that both business and investors suffer when they are too much ruled by the short term.

That said, it must be admitted that many of the longer-term investments required by sustainable development—such as toward new and renewable forms of energy or more eco-efficient forms of transport— are going to be pushed more by society at large than by business. And in doing this, society will act through its governments and through public opinion expressed in market choices. Thus if governments are to decrease greenhouse gas emissions, as they have agreed to do, then policies must be put in place to harness market forces to this goal.

Businesses will want to watch such trends carefully so as to be able to take advantage of new opportunities rather than suffer from imposed changes. Given that these trends will play out over years, rather than quarters, keeping up will itself require some long-term planning. Some companies will go further and actually campaign for long-term changes that reward eco-efficiency—while at the same time improving their own eco-efficiency to take advantage of these changes.

Markets are not inherently or necessarily short-term. But neither are markets abstract entities. They are no more than reflections of the cumulative choices of individuals. As civilization began to rely more on productive industry and less directly on renewable resources, individuals began to believe that the future would take care of itself. Rapid depletion of certain resources—forests, fish stocks, genetic resources, and so on—and growing pollution problems have shaken that belief. As society becomes more systematically concerned about the needs of future generations, we are confident that financial markets will reflect that concern.

• Efforts toward eco-efficiency by a company often reduce present earnings in favor of future potentials. Financial markets favor companies with high present earnings over those with future potentials.

This is largely true at present, but changing. In chapter 3 we identified 11 trends pushing companies toward greater eco-efficiency and suggested that there would be a bottom-line reward for moving in that direction. We believe that although there is an ebb and flow in these trends, the direction of movement is toward greater rewards for greater eco-efficiency.

But in the middle of the last decade of this century, there remains great uncertainty in business and markets about the validity of this belief. Will the United States dismantle its environmental regulatory structure? Will the new globalism allow multinational companies to relax environmental standards in countries where regulations are lax?

We have already argued that Americans will not accept a return to a time when some U.S. rivers were so polluted that they regularly caught fire, a time when whole towns had to be abandoned due to hazardous waste deposits. We have also found that multinationals are actually driving up environmental standards in the developing world by bringing their own home-country standards with them.

We are convinced that industrial-country markets will come to reward investments in eco-efficiency—provided that they are sound investments and are communicated effectively—in the same way they reward sound investments in research and development.

One key question is whether the emerging financial markets will reward eco-efficiency in the millions of small, domestic industries that have the greatest impact on the environment in developing nations. This will depend on the kinds of regulatory (and enforcement) regimes that emerge in these countries. A number of Asian and Latin American economies are catching up with some European ones in terms of most standards of "development." As education, health care, housing, and other standards of living improve, people are less willing to drink dirty water and breathe dirty air. Development, and the need for developing-world companies to compete in world markets, may encourage governments to establish frameworks that reward eco-efficiency. Then financial markets will begin to do the same.

• Given low resource prices and the ability of businesses to keep costs for much environmental damage "external" to their own balance sheets, the profitability of becoming eco-efficient is reduced. Eco-efficient companies are often not preferred by financial markets.

This is still all too true, but it does not represent a "market failure" by the financial markets. This assumption is similar to the preceding one, but is also dissimilar enough to be worth considering separately. Here the problem is not that eco-efficiency takes time and absorbs some profits. It is that it makes little sense to conserve resources if resources are cheap. Nor does it make strict bottom-line sense to limit pollution if a company pays little or nothing for the damage done by that pollution.

This is policy failure rather than market failure. Since society must pay—sooner and later—for squandered resources and pollution damages, it makes perfect sense to require that those with most direct control over these processes—polluting companies and those that use resources heavily—make the first payments. Although some of these payments will be for the damage done, in the spirit of the "Polluter Pays Principle" agreed by industrial countries more than three decades ago, most should be in the form of investments in cleaner processes to avoid future payments.

Ultimately, all costs incurred must be borne by the consumer—that is, the wider society from which policy changes must emerge. Successful companies will be those that, due to their eco-efficiency, pass along the lowest costs while staying ahead of changing policies.

The policy changes are simple but not easy. First, get rid of subsidies that in many countries encourage overuse of energy, fuels, forests, water, soils, pesticides, and fertilizer. Second, introduce market instruments that encourage pricing such that growing scarcities of resources are reflected in increasing prices—which does not happen in cases of subsidies and in cases where natural resources have no obvious owner. As important as these two steps is making sure that the use of pollution "sinks"—the atmosphere, bodies of water, and the soil—is priced appropriately. Regulations cover cases where resource use causes dangerous pollution, while taxes and charges encourage rational resource use and technology innovation.

The industrial nations have been "de-materializing" for some years now, producing more with less. Yet many of the biggest developing nations—such as China, India, Indonesia, and Brazil—are rapidly industrializing while not yet de-materializing. They are thus beginning to run short of such key resources as water, space on urban roads, and healthy air to breathe. Policy changes of the sort just described may become a prerequisite for the further industrial development of these nations.

• Sustainable development requires massive investments in developing countries. Financial markets put a high risk premium on investments in developing countries.

True, and the financial markets have been wise to assign such risk premiums, mainly to account for unpredictable changes in government policies. But the emerging market countries in the developing world are growing economically faster than the industrial world. So the higher risk has been offset by the promise of higher returns. The tragic countries remain those in parts of sub-Saharan Africa and of Asia where very high risk is matched by a promise of very low returns on all but a few specialized investments.

The more encouraging long-term news is of signs of diminishing risk in many developing countries. The newly industrialized Asian economies—Malaysia, Hong Kong, Singapore, South Korea, Taiwan, and Thailand—all created relatively safe investment markets in the eighties. China continues to struggle to do so, but attracts enormous investment due to explosive economic growth rates. South America, after the stagnant decade of the eighties, worked during the early nineties to build investor confidence. Much has been learned from the experiences of these countries.

The first lesson is that macroeconomic reform, though both difficult in its own right and necessary, is not enough. It must be followed by a second generation of reforms in legal systems, trade policy, tax policy, labor markets, privatization processes, and property registration.[3] To make matters worse, these reforms are all linked to one another and cannot be undertaken in isolation.

But experience has shown that such reform is possible and—as important in a democratizing world—that voters will support governments that undertake long-term reform programs if they are kept in the picture enough to have confidence in the process. These success stories make it very difficult for governments not undertaking such reforms to find reasonable explanations for their inactivity. From the early seventies, the developing world moved rapidly from blaming everything on colonialism, and then neo-colonialism, to blaming capitalism in general and multinational companies in particular. Today there is no one to blame for faulty policy regimes besides the governments and their stakeholders involved in policymaking. None of this is meant to ignore the fact that poor countries find if difficult to compete with rich countries in the marketplace. Bullying still occurs on steeply sloping playing fields. Much improvement in international trade and markets is needed.

As noted in chapter 2, in 1995 the World Bank predicted that economic growth rates in the developing world over the next decade could be 6 percent annually, twice that of the industrial world.[4] But the forecast assumes that developing-world governments will exercise economic discipline while continuing to liberalize their economies. We have pointed out that dozens of countries are establishing financial markets and privatization programs while liberalizing trade policies and foreign direct investment regimes.

Risk remains high in much of the developing world; but it is reduced where basic reforms are implemented. Returns may remain high, if reforming governments keep their nerve. And non-reforming governments are running out of excuses.

• High taxes on employment encourage labor productivity, thereby enhancing unemployment, while low resource prices discourage resource efficiency.

This is a controversial assumption. We cannot prove that high taxes on employment cause higher unemployment. But it does seem obvious that in a world where the cost of employing people is "artificially" high and the costs of resources are "artificially" low (especially where subsidized), business is going to be encouraged to use robots to add value to cheap resources. One report to a trans-Atlantic workshop on fiscal reform and the environment concluded that in Europe taxes on labor—rather than on resources or capital—had carried most of the burden for increased public spending over the past two decades.[5] The result was "a continuing system of tax disincentives for all decision makers, driving investment and consumption away from the socially desirable goals. Result: fewer jobs, more pollution."

Shifting the total tax burden away from things society values—such as employment and the creation of capital—and toward things society disdains—pollution and resource waste—must make sense. Business has been suspicious that if a government attempted this it would not be a tax shift but a tax addition. There is that danger. But as business becomes more involved in shaping polices, such a danger diminishes. Also, there is a tendency in much of the West away from high taxes for social services, and this tendency also decreases the danger.

Most developing countries need to reform their fiscal policies anyway, not only to improve them but to get more people to pay taxes. Indeed, they might be able to move toward a "taxing the negative" system more easily than Western nations, where fiscal systems are more entrenched.

• Accounting and reporting systems do not adequately convey potential environmental risks or opportunities. Financial markets are compelled to make decisions based on biased information.

True. And there are probably not a lot of accountants who would argue that in their daily work they do adequately convey environmental risks and opportunities. There are also many who would argue that this is not their job, that making it their job would require major changes in legal systems, and that this should not be done because the process of reflecting environmental risk and opportunity is fraught not only with financial uncertainty but also with scientific uncertainty. Environmental accounting is not a job for accountants, many might argue.

Having said this, we must add that the accounting profession is showing a great deal of energy and creativity in trying to make financial accounting better reflect the sorts of environmental realities that already or may soon affect business. Great progress is being made within corporations, where new systems of accounting for resources and pollution are being pioneered. The trailblazers face several problems, however, including the uncertainties mentioned above and their inability to run ahead of governments and business in these efforts.

So better accounting of this sort must await improved government policies, which would also encourage companies to demand of their accountants more accurate tallies of environmental effects, good and ill. If governments change national accounting systems, as they have been promising to do, to reflect resource net worth as well as income, companies will have to provide governments with more data on resource use. Much of this data must come from company accountants. To come full circle, efforts by accountants to devise new standards that reflect environmental reality will continue to encourage governments that improvements in accounting standards are possible and practical.

• Sustainable development is concerned with the importance of the future. Financial markets discount the future routinely and heavily.

This is the most difficult of our presumptions because it covers such a broad spectrum of financial, psychological, and even philosophical concerns. The issue not only concerns markets; it is a basic human reality. To persuade someone to accept a dollar in a year's time, rather than right now, you must pay that person more than one dollar in a year. That which we possess now is worth more than the chance, even the near certainty, of possessing an equal amount in the future. If we are going to use the item as a productive resource, it is obviously worth more because it starts producing and earning now rather than later. Even if it is to be consumed, its perceived reality today has a greater value than its possibility tomorrow. Any "market solutions" cannot ignore this truth.

The discount rate, here meaning the rate at which future cash flows are discounted, is an extremely complex economic concept that cannot be dealt with here in such a short space. Worrying about it goes in and out of vogue. This concern enjoyed fashion in the sixties, then declined, and was given a new lease on life by the concept of sustainable development.

Recently there have been calls for a zero discount rate for "environmental projects," or even a positive rate, which would make future cash flows more valuable than present flows, rather than less. There are several simple problems with this approach. The most obvious one is that it flies in the face of the reality just discussed. Environmental economist David Pearce and colleagues note two others.[6] In the real world, it would be impossible to separate "environmental" projects from other projects. Second, although high discount rates do encourage the harvesting of natural resources sooner rather than later, the effect of lower rates or positive rates is uncertain. They might encourage so much investment in the near future that a great deal of environmental degradation would occur. In other words, a lower, a zero, or a positive discount rate might encourage unsustainability.

So Pearce takes the bold step of proposing that where natural resources are involved, the criterion of sustainability be used in investment decisions: "Its appeal—particularly with regard to renewable resources—is evident," he maintains. "In many developing countries the stocks of such resources are below any reasonable estimate of what the long-run optimal stock is. In that event, it seems desirable that any investment policy that involves these resources should not permit a further fall in their stocks."

But this is true not only for developing countries. If environmental resources include clean air, clean water, productive seas, and a predictable climate, then investment policies in industrial countries should not deplete stocks of these or many other natural resources.

We have labored throughout this book to show how concerns for sustainable development and for efficient financial markets are moving together. But in conclusion we too must take a bold step and argue that sustainability should become a criterion of financial market decisions—as society values it more, as it becomes more obvious that civilization requires it.

Attempts more than 100 years ago to put concern for health and safety into business at first seemed intrusive and misguided. But society demanded it. Today, a lack of concern for health and safety by business would appear misguided.

The idea of giving financial markets a "sustainability reflex" may today appear novel, even radical, even intrusive and misguided. But markets, driven by forces both within and without, are developing such a reflex, which really is the reflex of a growing number of people. If it does not happen, or does not happen fast enough, an unsustainable human population will descend toward poverty and chaos.

Having offered our thoughts on the issue, from the perspective of a number of business leaders from around the world, we invite others in business, academia, or policy research to carry on this work. This book is only a part of a small beginning.

Appendix: Statement by Banks on the Environment and Sustainable Development

We, the undersigned, believe that human welfare, environmental protection and sustainable development depend on the commitment of governments, businesses and individuals. We recognise that the pursuit of economic growth and a healthy environment are inextricably linked. We further recognise that ecological protection and sustainable development are collective responsibilities and must rank among the highest priorities of all business activities, including banking. We will endeavour to ensure that our policies and business actions promote sustainable development: meeting the needs of the present without compromising those of the future.

(1) General Principles of Sustainable Development

(1.1.) We believe that all countries should work towards common environmental goals.

(1.2.) We regard sustainable development as a fundamental aspect of sound business management.

(1.3.) We believe that progress towards sustainable development can best be achieved by working within the framework of market mechanisms to promote environmental protection. We believe that there is a role for governments to provide the right signals to individuals and businesses, to promote behavioural changes in favour of effective environmental management through the conservation of energy and natural resources, whilst promoting economic growth.

(1.4.) We regard a versatile, dynamic financial services sector as an important contributor towards sustainable development.

(1.5.) We recognise that sustainable development is a corporate commitment and an integral part of our pursuit of good corporate citizenship. We are moving towards the integration of environmental considerations into internal banking operations and business decisions in a manner which enhances sustainable development.

(2) Environmental Management and Banks

(2.1.) We subscribe to the precautionary approach to environmental management, which strives to anticipate and prevent potential environmental degradation.

(2.2.) We expect, as part of our normal business practices, that our customers comply with all applicable local, national, and international environmental regulations. Beyond compliance, we regard sound environmental practices as one of the key factors demonstrating effective corporate management.

(2.3.) We recognise that environmental risks should be part of the normal checklist of risk assessment and management. As part of our credit risk assessment, we recommend, when appropriate, environmental impact assessments.

(2.4.) We will, in our domestic and international operations, endeavour to apply the same standards of environmental risk assessment.

(2.5.) We look to public institutions to conduct appropriate, up-to-date and comprehensive environmental assessments in ventures with them, and to share the results of those assessments with participating banks.

(2.6.) We intend to update our management practices, including accounting, marketing, risk assessment, public affairs, employee communications and training, to incorporate relevant developments in environmental management. We encourage banking research in these and related issues.

(2.7.) We will seek to ensure that in our internal operations we pursue the best practices in environmental management, including energy efficiency, recycling and waste minimisation. We will seek to form business relations with suppliers and sub-contractors who follow similarly high environmental standards.

(2.8.) We support and will develop suitable banking products and services designed to promote environmental protection, where there is a sound business rationale.

(2.9.) We recognise the need to conduct internal environmental reviews on a periodic basis to measure our operational activities against our environmental goals.

(3) Public Awareness and Communication

(3.1.) We will share information with customers, as appropriate, so that they may strengthen their own capacity to reduce environmental risk, and promote sustainable development.

(3.2.) We will foster openness and dialogue relating to environmental management with all relevant audiences, including governments, clients, employees, shareholders and the public.

(3.3.) We recommend that banks develop and publish a statement of their environmental policy and periodically report on its implementation.

(3.4.) We ask the United Nations Environment Programme to assist the industry by providing, within its capacity, relevant information relating to sustainable development.

(3.5.) We will periodically review the success in implementing this Statement and will revise it as appropriate.

(3.6.) We encourage other banks to support this Statement.

Signed in New York, May 1992. Available from Environment and Trade Unit, U.N. Environment Programme, Geneva.

Notes

Chapter 1

1. All figures from International Finance Corporation, *Emerging Stock Markets Factbook 1995* (Washington, D.C.: 1995).

2. Livingston Douglas, *The Bond Markets* (Chicago: Probus Publishing, 1995).

3. United Nations Population Fund, *State of the World's Population 1995* (New York: 1995).

4. World Bank, *World Development Report 1990* (New York: Oxford University Press, 1990).

5. World Commission on Environment and Development (WCED), *Our Common Future* (Oxford: Oxford University Press, 1987).

6. Ibid.

7. Stephan Schmidheiny with the Business Council for Sustainable Development (BCSD), *Changing Course: A Global Business Perspective on Development and the Environment* (Cambridge, Mass.: The MIT Press, 1992).

8. Estimate cited in Sean Kennedy, "Asia Search for Funds Has Problem of Recognition," *South China Morning Post*, November 9, 1994.

9. John Lawton and Robert May (eds.), *Extinction Rates* (Oxford: Oxford University Press, 1995).

10. Pam Woodall, "The Global Economy," *The Economist*, October 1, 1994.

11. Quoted in Michael Richardson, "Indonesia at Edge of Water Crisis," *International Herald Tribune*, November 26, 1994.

12. World Bank, *Global Economic Prospects and the Developing Countries* (Washington, D.C.: 1995).

13. Organisation for Economic Co-operation and Development, "Financial Flows to Developing Countries in 1994 (Preliminary Figures)," press release, Paris, June 21, 1995.

14. International Council of Voluntary Agencies, Eurostep, and Actionaid, "Reality of Aid," London, 1995.

15. Brad Gentry, Center for Environmental Law and Policy, Yale University, New Haven, Conn., personal communication, May 1992.

16. Hamish McRae, *The World in 2020—Power, Culture and Prosperity: A Vision of the Future* (London: HarperCollins, 1994).

17. Information on MSY and quotations from Colin Clark, *Mathematical Bioeconomics: The Optimal Management of Renewable Resources* (London: John Wiley & Sons, 1976).

18. Mark Mansley, "Achieving Sustainable Forestry: The Role of Capital Markets," Delphi International, London, 1995.

19. "The Green Keiretsu," *Tomorrow*, October–December 1994.

20. Schmidheiny, *Changing Course*.

21. The Hundred Group of Financial Directors Environmental Working Party, "Statement of Good Practice: Environmental Reporting in Annual Reports," Brentford, U.K., 1992.

22. Salomon Inc., "Environmental Policy Statement," New York, June 3, 1992.

23. Greenpeace information in this section from Dr. Jeremy Leggett, Director of Science and Climate Campaign, Greenpeace, London, personal communication, May 1995.

24. Quoted in F.W. Pointon, "Conflicts of Interest for Lending Bankers," in *The ACT Guide to Ethical Conflicts in Finance*, ed. Andreas Prindl and Bimal Prodham (Oxford: Blackwell Publishers, 1994).

25. Schmidheiny, *Changing Course*.

26. WCED, *Our Common Future*.

27. Quotes and survey data in the remainder of this section from UNCTAD Secretariat, "Incentives and Disincentives for the Adoption of Sustainable Development by Transnational Corporations," TD/B/ITNC/AC.1/3, Geneva, January 1995.

28. Andrew Marr, "Green Power in the World's Saloon Bar," *The Independent*, July 11, 1995.

29. Information on Shell plan and current status from "Shell on the Rocks," *The Economist*, June 24, 1995.

30. Novo Nordisk position and quote in next paragraph from John Elkington, "Sparring Partners," *The Guardian*, June 28, 1995.

31. "Human Rights," *The Economist*, June 3, 1995.

32. Franklin Research and IKEA example from ibid.

33. "Gallup Omnibus Survey Into Investor Attitudes," London, April 1995.

34. Ian Hamilton Fazey, "How the Dotty Line Can Give a Boost to the Bottom Line," *Financial Times*, January 3, 1995.

35. Aracruz Celulose, *Corporate Profile* (Rio de Janeiro: Aracruz Celulose, 1995).

36. David Webster, "The Free Market for Clean Air," *Business and Society Review*, June 22, 1994.

37. Royal Commission on Environmental Pollution, *Eighteenth Report: Transport and Environment* (London: Her Majesty's Stationery Office, 1994).

38. Judy Dempsey, "German Coalminers Celebrate Subsidy Victory," *Financial Times*, May 4, 1995.

39. Quotes in this and next paragraph from Schmidheiny, *Changing Course*.

40. Scott Vaughan, ed., *Greening Financial Markets* (Geneva: U.N. Environment Programme, 1995).

41. World Bank, *World Development Report 1992* (New York: Oxford University Press, 1992).

42. International Chamber of Commerce, *The Economy and the Environment, Business Brief No 1* (Paris: 1992).

43. Raymond Colitt, "Accounting for the Birds, Bees and Trees—Why Economic Indicators Must Reflect Degradation of Natural Resources," *Financial Times*, September 7, 1994.

44. Alan Day, ed., *The Annual Register: A Record of World Events 1993* (Burnt Mill, U.K.: Longmans, 1994).

45. Roberto de Andraca and Ken McCready, "Internalising Environmental Costs to Promote Eco-efficiency," BCSD, Geneva, 1994.

46. Richard House, "Rating Environmental Risk," *Institutional Investor*, March 1995.

Chapter 2

1. International Monetary Fund, *World Economic Outlook*, May 1993.

2. World Bank, *Global Economic Prospects and the Developing Countries, 1995* (Washington, D.C.: 1995).

3. U.N. Centre on Transnational Corporations, *World Investment Report, 1992* (New York: 1992).

4. Nicholas Parker, *Investing in Emerging Economies: A Business Guide to Official Assistance and Finance* (London: Economist Intelligence Unit, in cooperation with International Finance Corporation, 1993).

5. Cited in ibid.

6. Frances Williams, "World Trade News: Leap in Investment Flow to Developing Nations," *Financial Times*, March 8, 1995.

7. World Bank, *Global Economic Prospects and the Developing Countries*.

8. International Finance Corporation (IFC), *Emerging Stock Markets Factbook 1995* (Washington, D.C.: 1995).

9. Cited in Philip Coggan, "Wide Cracks in Road to Easy Riches," *Financial Times*, January 7, 1995.

10. World Institute for Development Economics Research, Study Group No 5, "Foreign Portfolio Investment in Emerging Equity Markets," United Nations University, Tokyo, 1994.

11. "The Lost Decades," *Euromoney*, June 1994.

12. Cited in Barry Riley, "Emerging Markets Survey," *Financial Times*, February 7, 1994.

13. World Bank, *Global Economic Prospects and the Developing Countries*.

14. Cited in Ben Edwards, "Searching for Green Roots," *Euromoney*, May 1994.

15. World Bank, *Latin America and the Caribbean: A Decade After the Debt Crisis* (Washington, D.C.: 1993).

16. U.N. Development Programme, *Human Development Report 1994* (New York: Oxford University Press, 1994).

17. M. Flaherty and C. Karnjanakesorn, "Marine Shrimp Aquaculture and Resource Degradation in Thailand," *Environmental Management*, Vol. 19, No. 1, 1995.

18. Martin Feldstein, "Global Capital Flows," *The Economist*, June 24, 1995.

19. John Gapper, "The Barings Collapse: SIB Urges Worldwide Regulation," *Financial Times*, March 9, 1995.

20. Quoted in Richard Lapper, "Regulators Aim to Gird the Globe," *Financial Times*, July 10, 1995.

21. Quoted in Richard Lapper, "Co-operation Urged Among Regulators," *Financial Times*, July 25, 1995.

22. David Pilling, "Bringing Reality to Shoppers' Paradise," *Financial Times*, July 11, 1995.

23. Andrew Jack, "Why Figures Do Not Add Up: Accounting Standards," *Financial Times*, January 20, 1995.

24. Philippines Business for the Environment, "Environmental Seminar for Bankers," Manila, February 15, 1994.

25. David Carey, "Getting Risk's Number," *Institutional Investor*, February 1995.

26. Ministry of Environment & Forests, *Environment Action Program India*, Government of India, New Delhi, 1993.

27. Carter Brandon, Asia Environment Division, World Bank, presentation to conference on "Financing Environmental Protection in Asia," Bangkok, December 2, 1993.

28. Harvey Yakovitz, Environment Directorate, Organisation for Economic Co-operation and Development (OECD), presentation to a workshop on "The Promotion of Access to and Dissemination of Information on Environmentally-sound Technologies," Korea Environmental Technology Research Institute, Seoul, December 1994.

29. Jeremy Eppel, Counsellor, Environment Directorate, OECD, Paris, personal communication, May 1995.

30. Mark Mansley and Nicholas Parker, "Financing the Transfer of Environmentally Sound Technology," U.N. Department for Policy Coordination and Sustainable Development, New York, January 1995.

31. The examples and figures in this section are from Nicholas Parker of Delphi International, London, private communications, and from Nicholas Parker, *Financing Cleaner Production* (Paris: United Nations Environment Programme, 1995).

32. Environment Department, "Privatization and Environmental Assessment: Issues and Approaches," *Environmental Assessment Sourcebook Update*, No. 6, World Bank, Washington, D.C., March 1994.

33. Nicholas Parker, "Financing Clean Energy Development in Emerging Economies: The Need for Innovation," *World Energy Council Journal*, July 1994.

34. The Delphi Group/SB Capital International, "India Energy & Environment Ventures Fund," Draft Offering Memorandum, London, February 1994.

35. Parker, "Financing Clean Energy Development."

36. Ibid.

37. Nicholas Parker, Delphi International, London, personal communication, August 1995.

38. International Finance Corporation, "Renewable Energy and Energy Efficiency Fund: Feasibility Study and Business Plan Development Terms of Reference," Washington, D.C., unpublished, 1995.

39. OECD, *International Economic Instruments and Climate Change* (Paris: 1993).

40. Ken McCready, President and Chief Executive Officer, TransAlta Utilities Corp., Edmonton, Alberta, Canada, personal communication.

Chapter 3

1. Royal Society for the Encouragement of the Arts, Manufactures, and Commerce (RSA), *Tomorrow's Company* (London: 1995).

2. Richard Barfield, "Shareholder Value: Managing for the Long Term," *Accountancy*, October 1991.

3. Thomas Copeland, Tim Koller, and Jack Murrin, *Valuation: Measuring and Managing the Value of Companies* (New York: John Wiley & Sons, 1994).

4. UNCTAD Secretariat, "Incentives and Disincentives for the Adoption of Sustainable Development by Transnational Corporations," TD/B/ITNC/AC.1/3, Geneva, January 1995.

5. Adrian Wooldridge, "A Survey of Multinationals," *The Economist*, June 24, 1995.

6. British Petroleum, *BP in the Community* (London: 1995).

7. Wooldridge, "Survey of Multinationals."

8. Franceska van Dijk, "Beyond the Green Sell," *EEMA Review* (Journal of European Environmental Management Association), May 1995.

9. See, for example, Daryl Ditz, Janet Ranganathan, and R. Darryl Banks, *Green Ledgers: Case Studies in Corporate Environmental Accounting* (Washington, D.C.: World Resources Institute, 1995).

10. All Michigan study citations in this section from Stuart Hart and Gautam Ahuja, "Does It Pay To Be Green?" University of Michigan, Ann Arbor, September 1994.

11. Results and quotes from Mark Cohen et al., "Environmental and Financial Performance: Are They Related?" Investor Responsibility Research Center, Washington, D.C., April 1995.

12. Hart and Ahuja, "Does It Pay To Be Green?"

13. Dow Chemical Company, *Environmental Progress Report 1993* (Midland, Mich.: 1993).

14. Monsanto Company, *Environmental Annual Review* (St. Louis, Mo.: 1991).

15. Action: Employees in the Community, "Business on Board," London 1995

16. "Charity Begins at Work," *The Economist*, December 17, 1994.

17. Noah Walley and Bradley Whitehead, "It's Not Easy Being Green," *Harvard Business Review*, May–June 1994.

18. Richard Clarke et al., "The Challenge of Going Green," *Harvard Business Review*, July-August 1994.

19. Frances Cairncross, *Green, Inc: A Guide to Business and the Environment* (London: Earthscan, 1995).

20. John Elkington, "On Hanging Judges," *Tomorrow*, July–September 1995.

21. Dale Martin, Environmental Effectiveness Manager, "Environmental Planning: Balancing Environmental Commitments with Economic Realities," DuPont, Wilmington, Del., 1993.

22. Union Pacific, "Union Pacific Corporation and the Environment," Bethlehem, Pa., November 1993.

23. DuPont data and quotes in this section from Martin, "Environmental Planning."

24. Baxter, *Environmental Performance Report 1993* (Deerfield, Ill.: 1993).

25. Stephan Schmidheiny with the Business Council for Sustainable Development, *Changing Course: A Global Business Perspective on Development and the Environment* (Cambridge, Mass.: The MIT Press, 1992).

26. RSA, *Tomorrow's Company*.

27. Stephen Prowse, "Corporate Governance in an International Perspective," BIS Economic Paper No. 41, Bank for International Settlements, Basel, Switzerland, July 1994.

28. Jeffrey Gates and Jamil Saghir, "Employee Stock Ownership Plans (ESOPs): Objectives, Practice and Experience," World Bank Discussion Paper, Washington, D.C., forthcoming.

29. Michael Porter, "Capital Choice: Changing the Way America Invests in Industry," a joint research project by the *Harvard Business Review* and the Council on Competitiveness, 1992.

Chapter 4

1. Forests Monitor, letter to fund managers, August 6, 1993, Plymouth, U.K.

2. Quote here and in next paragraph from Peter Knight, "Campaign to Fell Pulp Producer," *Financial Times*, August 11, 1993.

3. Heinz Zimmermann and Mark Tapely, *Finanzmarkt Schweiz—Strukturen im Wandel* [Financial Market Switzerland—Changing Structures] (St. Gallen, Switzerland: University of St. Gallen, 1989).

4. Edward Tasch and Stephen Viederman, "New Concepts of Fiduciary Responsibility," in *Steering Business Toward Sustainability*, ed. Fritjof Capra and Gunter Pauli (Tokyo: United Nations University Press, 1995).

5. Anne Simpson, "The Greening of Global Investment: How the Environment, Ethics and Politics Are Reshaping Strategies," Economist Publications Special Report No. 2108 (London: The Economist Publications, 1991).

6. Data in this paragraph from "Rückzug der Privatanleger von der Londoner Börse" [Retreat of private investors from the London Stock Exchange], *Neue Zürcher Zeitung*, December 3/4, 1994.

7. Bank Julius Bär, "Marktübersicht Schweiz 1994" [Market Overview Switzerland], Zurich, 1994.

8. "When George Soros Meets Granny Smith," *The Economist*, April 22, 1995.

9. Bevis Longstreth, *Modern Investment Management and the Prudent Man Rule* (New York: Oxford University Press, 1986), as quoted in Tasch and Viederman, "New Concepts."

10. John Vidal, "Clean Money Talks," *Guardian* (London), May 17, 1995.

11. "Morals Maketh Money: Ethical Investing Is Now a Big Business. But It Is Not Yet a Force for Good," *The Economist*, September 3, 1994.

12. "Now There is a Fund for Sinners, Too," *Sunday Times* (London), May 21, 1995.

13. Mark Campanale, National Provident Institution, London, personal communication, June 1995.

14. Louis Knowles, "Social Investing Rolls Along," *Foundation News and Commentary*, March/April 1995.

15. Tasch and Viederman, "New Concepts."

16. Interfaith Center for Corporate Responsibility, New York, personal communication, July 1993.

17. Simpson, "The Greening of Global Investment."

18. Tessa Tennant, Head of Environmental and Ethical Research, National Provident Institution, London, personal communication, May 1995.

19. Ronald Watson, "The Controversy Over Targeted Investing," *Compensation & Benefits Management*, Winter 1995.

20. Tasch and Viederman, "New Concepts."

21. Quoted in Jeremy Leggett, "Climate Change: How Bad Is It? What Is Being Done? What Needs To Be Done?" Greenpeace pamphlet, London, 1994.

22. Details in this section of Indonesian rain forest and Edinburgh Java Trust from "Pensions Linked to Forest Scandal," *Sunday Times* (London), August 28, 1994.

23. Open letter from Mike Balfour, Edinburgh Fund Managers, Edinburgh, U.K., August 25, 1994.

24. Mike Balfour, Edinburgh Fund Managers, Edinburgh, U.K., personal communication, July 1995.

25. Extel Financial and Business in the Environment, *City Analysts and the Environment* (London: Business in the Environment, 1994).

26. Quotes here and in the remainder of this section from Mark Mansley, Delphi International, London, personal communication, and from Mark Mansley, "Questions of Ethics," *Pensions Management*, July 1995.

27. Jonathan V. Snyder and Charles H. Collins, *The Performance Impact of an Environmental Screen* (Boston: Winslow Management Company, 1993).

28. Survey results in this section from Extel Financial and Business in the Environment, *City Analysts and the Environment.*

29. Report results in remainder of this section from Mark Mansley, *The Long Term Financial Risks to the Carbon Fuel Industry from Climate Change* (London: Delphi International, 1994).

30. "Environmental Reporting and Disclosures," European Federation of Financial Analysts' Societies, Paris, September 1994.

31. Richard House, presentation at Banking on the Environment Conference, London, July 4, 1995.

Chapter 5

1. Michael Rubino, International Finance Corporation, Washington, D.C., personal communication, July 1995.

2. "The Basic Documents of the European Bank for Reconstruction and Development," Paris, May 19, 1990 (entered into force March 28, 1991).

3. "Rückzug der Privatanleger von der Londoner Börse" [Retreat of private investors from the London Stock Exchange], *Neue Zürcher Zeitung,* December 3/4, 1994.

4. Mirabile case based on Michael Kupin, "New Alterations of the Lender Liability Landscape: CERCLA After the Fleet Factors Decision," *Real Estate Law Journal,* Winter 1991.

5. Mary Aronov, "Developments in Lender Liability Under Environmental Laws," *Real Estate Finance Journal,* Fall 1992.

6. Fleet Factors case based on Michael Buckley and Craig Johns, "Lender Liability Under CERCLA: A New Age of Discontent," *Commercial Investment Real Estate Journal,* Winter 1992.

7. Buckley and Johns, "Lender Liability under CERCLA."

8. William D. Evans, Jr., "Judicial Relief from Superfund Claims: Some Good News, Possibly Fleeting for Bankers," *Banking Law Journal,* January-February 1994.

9. "Bank Group Focusses on E-liability Issues," *Environment Today,* April 1994.

10. Scott Vaughan, ed., *Greening Financial Markets* (Geneva: United Nations Environment Programme, 1995).

11. European Commission, "Remedying Environmental Damage," Com(93)47, Brussels, March 1993.

12. Lesley Grayson et al., *Business and Environmental Accountability: An Overview and Guide to the Literature* (Letchworth, U.K.: Technical Communications (Publishing) Ltd., 1993).

13. List in remainder of this section from Vaughan, *Greening Financial Markets.*

14. British Bankers' Association, "Banks and the Environment," London, 1993.

15. Hilary Thompson, Environmental Management Unit, National Westminster Bank, personal communication, May 1995.

16. Angus Foster, "Brazil Seeks a 'Sustainable' Amazon," *Financial Times,* April, 19, 1995.

17. Hilary Thompson, Environmental Management Unit, National Westminster Bank, personal communication, June 1995.

18. British Bankers' Association, "Lenders & Environmental Liability," London, September 1993.

19. U.K. Department of Trade and Industry, "Small and Medium Sized Enterprise Statistics for the United Kingdom, 1993," London, June 1995.

20. Data on small businesses in Latin America here and in next paragraph from Ernst Brugger et al., *The Cutting Edge* (Niederurnen, Switzerland: FUNDES, 1994).

21. Brian Collett, "Green Handouts for Small Companies," *The Times* (London), July 19, 1995.

22. Franz Knecht, Vice President, Swiss Bank Corporation, Basel, Switzerland, personal communication, March 1995.

23. National Westminster Bank plc, "Response to the EU's Green Paper on Remedying Environmental Damage," London, October 1993.

24. Quote and examples in next paragraph from Nicholas Lenssen and David Malin Roodman, "Making Better Buildings," in Lester R. Brown et al., *State of the World 1995* (New York: W.W. Norton & Company, 1995).

25. Deutsche Bank and National Westminster Bank from Thompson, personal communications.

26. All details on Coop Bank from Lindsay Vincent, "The Co-op Crusader—Terry Thomas," *The Observer* (London), April 9, 1995.

27. "1993 Ethical Environment Statement for Sbn Bank Denmark," *Social and Environmental Accounting,* September 1994.

28. This and next paragraph based on Mark Mansley, Delphi International, London, personal communication, June 1995.

29. Banking members of Working Group on Financial Markets, World Business Council for Sustainable Development (WBCSD), personal communications.

30. Raymond Mgadzah, "Aston Gets Its Assets in Gear," *The Independent* (London), January 11, 1995.

31. A.N.M. Wahid, "The Grameen Bank and Poverty Alleviation in Bangladesh: Theory, Evidence and Limitations," *American Journal of Economics and Sociology,* Vol. 53, No. 1, 1994.

32. Details and quote from "Global Grass-roots Banking" (editorial), *New York Times,* July 27, 1995.

33. Details and quotes in this section from Karen Horn, "Banking in the 21st Century: From Supermarkets to Satellites," paper prepared for Digital's Bankers to Bankers conference, Istanbul, October 1994.

34. Details in this and next paragraph from "Taking Microchips to Townships," *The Economist,* July 8, 1995.

35. WBCSD Working Group members.

36. Jeremy Leggett, "Climate Change and the Financial Sector: Taking Bearings in the Greenhouse," prepared for Greenpeace conference, Berlin Conference Center, March 26, 1995.

37. Vaughan, *Greening Financial Markets.*

38. U.N. Round-Table Meeting on Commercial Banks and the Environment, Geneva, September 26–27, 1994.

Chapter 6

1. Jeremy Leggett, "Who Will Underwrite the Hurricane?" *New Scientist,* August 7, 1993.

2. "A Report on the Finding of the Visit from the Lloyd's Underwriters Non-Marine Association to the First Conference of Parties of the United Nations Framework Convention on Climate Change," London, unpublished, March 1995.

3. Intergovernmental Panel on Climate Change, *Climate Change: The IPCC Scientific Assessment* (New York: Cambridge University Press, 1990).

4. John Snyder and W. Dolson Smith, "Environmental/Asbestos Liability Exposures: A P/C Industry Black Hole," *BestWeek,* March 28, 1994.

5. Ibid.

6. Quote and estimate of annual costs from M. McGavick, "Superfund: A Noble Idea Fallen on Hard Times," *Environment Strategy America 1994/5,* ed. William K. Reilly (London: Campden Publishing, 1994).

7. Richard House, "Balance Sheet Poison," *Institutional Investor,* August 1993.

8. Eugene Linden, "Burned by Warming," *Time Magazine,* March 14, 1994.

9. Herbert Fromme, "Munich Re Plea for Catastrophe Action," *Lloyd's List,* April 23, 1993.

10. "Global Warming: Element of Risk," Swiss Re special report, Zurich, 1994.

11. "Report on visit from the Lloyd's Underwriters Non-Marine Association."

12. "Global Warming: Element of Risk."

13. "The Impact of Changing Weather Patterns on Property Insurance," Chartered Insurance Institute special report, London, May 1994.

14. Based on Greenpeace International, "Climate Change and the Insurance Industry: Solidarity Among the Risk Community," London, January 1993, and on Dr. Jeremy Leggett, Director of Science and Climate Campaign, Greenpeace, London, personal communication, May 1995.

15. "Report on the Visit from the Lloyd's Underwriters Non-Marine Association."

16. Am Re description and quote in this section from "Commercializing Emerging Environmental Technologies," *Forbes*, November 7, 1994.

17. UNI Storebrand details in this section from Carlos Joly, Senior Vice President, UNI Storebrand, personal communication, August 1995.

18. Elizabeth Dowdeswell, Executive Director, U.N. Environment Programme (UNEP), statement at the 1st Session of the Conference of the Parties to the U.N. Framework Convention on Climate Change, Berlin, March 28, 1995.

19. Kenneth Maguire, UNEP, Geneva, personal communication, August 1995.

20. Economist Intelligence Unit, *Environmental Finance: Evaluating Risk and Exposure in the 1990s* (London: 1993).

Chapter 7

1. Dutch and U.K. examples from Frances Cairncross, *Green, Inc: A Guide to Business and the Environment* (London: Earthscan, 1995).

2. "A Green Account—A Growing Number of Companies Publish Environmental Accounts," *The Economist*, September 4, 1993.

3. "Price Waterhouse Study Focuses on Environmental Practices," *Environmental Manager*, May 1995.

4. Auditing Practices Board, "Future Development of Auditing: A Paper to Promote Public Debate," Accountancy Books, London, 1992.

5. International Auditing Practices Committee, "The Audit Profession and the Environment," International Federation of Accountants, New York, May 1995.

6. Daryl Ditz, Janet Ranganathan, and R. Darryl Banks, *Green Ledgers: Case Studies in Corporate Environmental Accounting* (Washington, D.C.: World Resources Institute, 1995).

7. Jim Kelly and Richard Lapper, "Plan for Global Accounting Standards," *Financial Times*, July 12, 1995.

8. Rob Gray et al., *Accounting for the Environment* (London: Paul Chapman, 1993).

9. Daniel Rubenstein, *Environmental Accounting for the Sustainable Corporation* (Westport, Conn.: Quorum Books, 1994).

10. IASC standards and SEC acceptance from David Cairns, "World Moves Closer to International Standards," *Financial Times*, May 11, 1995.

11. Kelly and Lapper, "Plan for Global Accounting Standards."

12. Gray et al., *Accounting for the Environment.*

13. Rubenstein, *Environmental Accounting.*

14. Ibid.

15. Wouter van Dieren, *Taking Nature into Account* (New York: Springer-Verlag, 1995).

16. Industrial-country progress and U.N. efforts with developing countries from Cairncross, *Green, Inc.*

17. Gray et al., *Accounting for the Environment.*

18. Lesley Grayson et al., *Business and Environmental Accountability: An Overview and Guide to the Literature* (Letchworth, U.K.: Technical Communications (Publishing) Ltd., 1993).

19. *SEC Accounting Rules*, Reg §229.303, Item 303, Amended by Release Numbers AS-306, FR-2, FR-7 and FR-30, Commerce Clearing House, Chicago, 1992 (regular updating service).

20. Financial Accounting Standards Board, *Accounting Standards—Current Texts* (Norwalk, Conn.: 1995); John Salavich, "Show and Tell: New Developments Impacting the Disclosure of Environmental Liabilities," *Journal of Environmental Permitting,* Summer 1994.

21. Working Document for European Commission Accounting Advisory Forum, "Environmental Issues in Financial Reporting" (draft), Brussels, 1994.

22. Grayson et al., *Business and Environmental Accountability.*

23. Ibid.

24. "How Green is My Balance Sheet? Environmental Accounting," *The Economist,* September 3, 1994.

25. Rubenstein, *Environmental Accounting.*

26. British Standards Institution, "Specification for Environmental Management Systems," pamphlet, London, 1992.

27. "International Voluntary Environmental Management Standards Evolve as ISO 14000 Delegates Wrap Up Oslo Conclave," *E-wire,* July 25, 1995.

28. Peter Knight, "Second Push for Green Reporting," *Financial Times,* November 16, 1994.

29. Ruth Hillary, *The Eco-management and Audit Scheme—A Practical Guide* (Letchworth, U.K.: Technical Communications (Publishing) Ltd., 1993).

30. Working Document for European Commission, "Environmental Issues in Financial Reporting."

31. Information on ACBE and quote in next paragraph from Advisory Committee on Business and Environment, "Report of the Financial Sector Working Group," Department of Trade and Industry and Department of the Environment, London, 1993.

32. Quoted in Roger Adams, "The Coming Convergence of Environmental and Accounting Issues," *Environmental Accounting and Auditing Reporter,* June 1995.

33. Japanese Ministry of Trade and Industry, *Voluntary Plan in Relation to the Environment* (Tokyo: 1992).

34. K. Kokubu, K. Tominasu, and T. Yamagami, *Green Reporting in Japan: Accountability and Legitimacy* (London: Centre for Social and Environmental Accounting Research, 1994).

Chapter 8

1. Ratings and cost estimates in next paragraph from Max Deml, Jörg Baumgartner, and Luc Bobikiewicz, *Gruenes Geld* [Green money] (Vienna: Service Fachverlag, 1994).

2. We rely heavily in this chapter on the work of Bob Ray at Moody's Investors Services in New York and David Lascelles of the *Financial Times* in London.

3. Quoted in Richard House, "Rating Environmental Risk," *Institutional Investor*, March 1995.

4. Kenneth Gooding, "Pechiney Sees Cloud Over US Beverage Can Sector," *Financial Times*, May 3, 1995.

5. Data and quote from Peter Elstob, editor of *Credit Ratings in Emerging Markets*, cited in Richard Lapper, "Growth in Rating Agencies Serving Emerging Markets," *Financial Times*, November 2, 1994.

6. Scott Vaughan (ed.), *Greening Financial Markets* (Geneva: United Nations Environment Programme, 1995).

7. Details on Scottish Nuclear rating and quotes in this section from Centre For the Study of Financial Innovation, *An Environmental Risk Rating for Scottish Nuclear* (London: 1995).

8. David Lascelles, "Business and the Environment: Credit Where Credit Is Due—An Ambitious Attempt to Rate Companies According to Their Greenness," *Financial Times*, August 10, 1994.

9. Lucy Roberts, "Index Will Give Companies a 'Green' Rating," *The Independent* (London), May 31, 1995.

10. Kelly Bernbeck, Business in the Environment, London, personal communication, June 1995.

11. Working Group on Financial Markets, World Business Council for Sustainable Development (WBCSD), personal communication.

12. Lascelles, "Business and the Environment."

13. Bernbeck, personal communication.

14. Anne Simpson, "The Greening of Global Investment: How the Environment, Ethics and Politics Are Reshaping Strategies," Special Report No. 2108 (London: The Economist Publications, 1991).

15. WBCSD Working Group members, personal communications, May-July 1995.

Part III

1. J.B. Bracewell-Milnes, "Are Equity Markets Short-sighted? Short-termism and Its Critics," Institute of Directors, London, 1987.

2. Paul Marsh, "Short-termism on Trial," a report commissioned by the International Fund Managers Association, London Business School, 1990.

3. Paul Holden and Sarath Rajapatirana, *Unshackling the Private Sector: A Latin American Story* (Washington, D.C.: World Bank, 1995).

4. World Bank, *Global Economic Prospects and the Developing Countries, 1995* (Washington, D.C.: 1995).

5. Lorenz Jarass and Gustav Obermair, "More Jobs, Less Pollution: A Tax Policy for an Improved Use of Production Factors," report to workshop on Transatlantic Fiscal Reform and the Environment, World Resources Institute and Center for Energy Conservation and Environmental Technology, Amsterdam, June 6, 1994.

6. Description here and quotes in next paragraph from David Pearce et al., *Sustainable Development: Economics and Environment in the Third World* (London: Earthscan, 1990).

Glossary of Acronyms

ABT	American Bank and Trust
ACBE	Advisory Committee on Business and the Environment (UK)
ADB	Asian Development Bank
BCSD	Business Council for Sustainable Development
BIS	Bank for International Settlements
BOT	build-operate-transfer
BP	British Petroleum
CEO	chief executive officer
CERCLA	Comprehensive Environmental Response, Compensation and Liability Act (US)
CERES	Coalition for Environmentally Responsible Economies
CSFI	Centre for the Study of Financial Innovation (UK)
DCF	discounted cash flow
EAS	Ethical Accounting Statement (Sbn Bank, Denmark)
EBRD	European Bank for Reconstruction and Development
EITF	Emerging Issues Task Force (FASB)
EMAS	Eco-Management and Audit Scheme (EU)
EPA	Environmental Protection Agency (US)
ERMR	Environmental Risk Management Rating
ESCos	energy service companies
ESOP	employee stock ownership plan
EU	European Union
EVC	European Vinyls Corporation (Netherlands)
FASB	Financial Accounting Standards Board (US)

FDI	foreign direct investment
FFC	Fleet Factors Corporation (US)
GATT	General Agreement on Tariffs and Trade
GBN	Green Business Network
GEEMF	Global Environment Emerging Markets Fund
GNP	gross national product
IASC	International Accounting Standards Committee
ICC	International Chamber of Commerce
IFC	International Finance Corporation
IMF	International Monetary Fund
IRRC	Investor Responsibility Research Center (US)
ISO	International Organisation for Standardisation
JI	joint implementation
M&A	mergers and acquisitions
MB	Mellon Bank (US)
MBT	Maryland Bank and Trust (US)
MDA	Management's Discussion and Analysis
MSY	maximum sustainable yield
NAEF	North American Environmental Fund
NEFCO	Nordic Environmental Finance Corporation
NPI	National Provident Institution (UK)
ODA	official development assistance
OECD	Organisation for Economic Co-operation and Development
OPIC	Overseas Private Investment Corporation (US)
PIOR	Pollutants Input-Output Reconciliation
PIRC	Pensions and Investment Research Consultants (UK)
PPP	polluter pays principle
PRP	potentially responsible party
PV	photovoltaics
R&D	research and development
ROE	return on equity
ROI	Risk & Opportunity Intelligence (UK)

S&P	Standard & Poor's
SBA	Small Business Administration (US)
SBC	Swiss Bank Corporation
SEC	Securities and Exchange Commission (US)
SMEs	small and medium-sized enterprises
SNAs	standard national accounts
SPWI	Swainsboro Print Works Inc. (US)
SYBERR	System Based Environmental Risk Rating
TCI	Turco Coatings Inc. (US)
UNCTAD	United Nations Conference on Trade and Development
UNEP	United Nations Environment Programme
UNISAR	U.N. Intergovernmental Working Group of Experts on International Standards of Accounting and Reporting
VOC	volatile organic compound
WBCSD	World Business Council for Sustainable Development
WCED	World Commission on Environment and Development
WICE	World Industry Council for the Environment

Selected Bibliography
and Further Reading

Aaheim, A., and K. Nyborg. "On the Interpretation and Applicability of a 'Green National Product'." *Review of Income and Wealth.* March 1995.

Adams, W.M., and D.H.L. Thomas. "Mainstream Sustainable Development—The Challenge of Putting Theory into Practice." *Journal of International Development.* November-December 1993.

Barde, J.P., and D. Pearce. *Valuing the Environment: Six Case Studies.* London: Earthscan Publications, 1991.

Bartelmus, P.T. *Environment, Growth and Development: The Concepts and Strategies of Sustainability.* London: Routledge, 1994.

Batabyal, A.A. "Development, Trade, and the Environment: Which Way Now?" *Ecological Economics.* May 1995.

Bennett, S.J., R. Freierman, and S. George. *Corporate Realities and Environmental Truths: Strategies for Leading Your Business in the Environmental Era.* New York: John Wiley, 1993.

Blumenfeld, J. "Institutions—The United Nations Commission on Sustainable Development." *Environment.* December 1994.

Brookfield, H.C., and Y. Byron, eds. *South-East Asia's Environmental Future: The Search for Sustainability.* Oxford: Oxford University Press, 1993.

Brown, L.R., et al. *State of the World 1995.* New York: W.W. Norton & Company, 1995.

Brugger E., et al. *The Cutting Edge.* Niederurnen, Switzerland: FUNDES, 1994.

Cairncross, F. *Green, Inc: A Guide to Business and the Environment.* London: Earthscan Publications, 1995.

Cameron, J., and T. O'Riordan, eds. *Interpreting the Precautionary Principle.* London: Earthscan Publications, 1994.

Capra, F., and G. Pauli, eds. *Steering Business Toward Sustainability.* Tokyo: United Nations University Press, 1995.

Carew-Reid, J., et al., eds. *Strategies for National Sustainable Development: A Handbook for Their Planning and Implementation.* London: Earthscan Publications, 1994.

Caruso, A. "Le Nazioni Unite e L'azione per lo Sviluppo All'alba del Terzo Millennio: L'agenda per lo Sviluppo" [The United Nations and actions for development on the threshold of the third millennium: The agenda for development]. *Comunita Internazionale.* Vol. 49, No. 4, 1994.

Choudhury, M.A. "Ethics and Economics: A View from Ecological Economics." *International Journal of Social Economics.* Vol. 22, No. 3, 1995.

Clark, C. *Mathematical Bioeconomics: The Optimal Management of Renewable Resources.* London: John Wiley & Sons, 1976.

Cohen, R. "Growth is Development, Distribution is Politics." *Research in Economic Anthropology.* Vol. 15, 1994.

Common, M.S., R.K. Blamey, and T.W. Norton. "Sustainability and Environmental Valuation." *Environmental Values.* Winter 1993.

Daly, H. E. "Fostering Environmentally Sustainable Development: Four Parting Suggestions for the World Bank." *Ecological Economics.* August 1994.

de Andraca, R., and K. McCready. "Internalising Environmental Costs to Promote Eco-efficiency." Geneva: Business Council for Sustainable Development, 1994.

Ditz, D., J. Ranganathan, and R.D. Banks. *Green Ledgers: Case Studies in Corporate Environmental Accounting.* Washington, D.C.: World Resources Institute, 1995.

Dixon, J.A., et al. *Economic Analysis of Environmental Impacts.* London: Earthscan Publications, 1994.

Dutch Committee for Long-Term Environmental Policy, ed. *The Environment: Towards a Sustainable Future.* Dordrecht: Kluwer Academic Publishers, 1994.

Ekins, P. "'Limits to Growth' and 'Sustainable Development'—Grappling with Ecological Realities." *Ecological Economics.* December 1993.

Elkington, J., and T. Burke. *The Green Capitalists: Industry's Search for Environmental Excellence.* London: Gollancz, 1987.

Friends of the Earth. *Planning for the Planet: Sustainable Development Policies for Local and Strategic Plans.* London: Friends of the Earth, 1994.

Garrity, M., and L.A. Picard, eds. *Policy Reform for Sustainable Development in Africa: The Institutional Imperative.* London: Lynne Rienner Publishers, 1994.

Ghai, D., ed. *Development and Environment: Sustaining People and Nature.* Oxford: Blackwell, 1994.

Gore, A. *Earth in the Balance.* London: Earthscan Publications, 1992.

Gray, R. *Accounting for the Environment.* London: Paul Chapman, 1993.

Gray, R. *Corporate Social Reporting: Accounting and Accountability.* London: Prentice Hall International, 1987.

Hamilton, K. "Green Adjustments to GDP." *Resources Policy.* September 1994.

Heyes, A.G., and C. Liston Heyes. "Sustainable Resource Use: The Search for Meaning." *Energy Policy.* January 1995.

Holden, P., and S. Rajapatirana. *Unshackling the Private Sector: A Latin American Story.* Washington, D.C.: World Bank, 1995.

Kleiner, A. "What Does It Mean To Be Green?" *Harvard Business Review*. July/August 1992.

Lanoie, P., B. Laplante, and G.A. Tanguay. "La Firme et l'Environnement" [The firm and the environment]. *Actualite Economique*. June 1994.

London, C. "Les Aides Financieres en Faveur de la Protection de l'Environnement" [Subsidies for environmental protection]. *Droit et Pratique du Commerce International*. Vol. 20, No. 2, 1994.

Macve, R., and A. Carey, eds. "Business, Accountancy and the Environment: A Policy and Research Agenda." London: Institute of Chartered Accountants in England and Wales. 1992.

Makower, J. *Beyond the Bottom Line: Putting Social Responsibility to Work for Your Business and the World*. New York: Simon & Schuster, 1994.

Markandya, A., and J. Richardson. *The Earthscan Reader in Environmental Economics*. London: Earthscan Publications, 1992.

Maxwell, R.S. "The Challenge of Environmental Technology Development." *Greener Management International*. April 1994.

McCulloch, A., and J. Moxen. "Government Support for Voluntary Improvement in the Environmental Standards of the UK Business Community." *Greener Management International*. April 1994.

Owen, D., ed. *Green Reporting: Accountancy and the Challenge of the Nineties*. London: Chapman and Hall, 1992.

Parker, K. "Economics, Sustainable Growth and Community." *Environmental Values*. Autumn 1993.

Pearce, D., A. Markandya, and E.B. Barbier. *Blueprint for a Green Economy*. London: Earthscan Publications, 1994.

Pearce D., et al. *Sustainable Development: Economics and Environment in the Third World*. London: Earthscan, 1990.

Peattie, K. *Green Marketing*. London: Pitman, 1992.

Pfeffer, J. "Bringing the Environment Back In—The Social Context of Business Strategy." United Nations Library on Transnational Corporations, Vol. 4—Transnational Corporations and Business Strategy. London: Routledge, 1993.

Radke, V. "Nachhaltige Entwicklung—Okonomische Implikationen [Sustainable development—economic implications]. *Jahrbucher fur Nationalokonomie und Statistik*, May 1995.

Rainbow, S. *Green Politics*. Oxford: Oxford University Press, 1993.

Redclift, M. "Sustainable Development—Needs, Values, Rights." *Environmental Values*. Spring 1993.

Reidenbach, R.E., and D.P. Robin. *Ethics and Profits: A Convergence of Corporate America's Economic and Social Responsibilities*. New York: Prentice Hall, 1989.

Repetto, R. "Accounting for Environmental Assets." *Scientific American*. June 1992.

Rubenstein, D.B. *Environmental Accounting for the Sustainable Corporation: Strategies and Techniques*. Westport, Conn.: Quorum Books, 1994.

Ryall, C., and S. Riley. "Green Investment: An Incentive for Business." *Greener Management International.* January 1994.

Scherhorn, G. "Consumers' Concern About the Environment and Its Impact on Business." *Journal of Consumer Policy.* Vol. 16, No. 2, 1993.

Schmidheiny, S., with the Business Council for Sustainable Development. *Changing Course: A Global Business Perspective on Development and the Environment.* Cambridge, Mass.: The MIT Press, 1992.

Skolimowski, H. "In Defence of Sustainable Development." *Environmental Values.* February 1995.

Smart, B. *Beyond Compliance.* Washington, D.C.: World Resources Institute, 1992.

Smith, D., ed. *Business and the Environment: Implications of the New Environmentalism.* London: Paul Chapman, 1992.

Smith, N.C. *Morality and the Market: Consumer Pressure for Corporate Accountability.* London: Routledge, 1991.

Solow, R. "An Almost Practical Step Towards Sustainability." *Resources Policy.* September 1993.

Solow, R., and L.L. Pasinetti, eds. *Economic Growth and the Structure of Long-term Development.* London: Macmillan Press, 1994.

Stetting, L., K.E. Svendsen, and E. Yndgaard, E., eds., *Global Change and Transformation.* Copenhagen: Handelshojskolens Forlag, 1993.

van Dieren, W. *Taking Nature into Account.* New York: Springer-Verlag, 1995.

Vaughan, S., ed. *Greening Financial Markets.* Geneva: United Nations Environment Programme, 1995.

Waller-Hunter, J.H. "The Commission on Sustainable Development: A Mandate for Change." *Natural Resources Forum.* November 1994.

Welford, R. *Environmental Strategy and Sustainable Development: The Corporate Challenge for the 21st Century.* London: Routledge, 1994.

World Commission on Environment and Development. *Our Common Future.* Oxford: Oxford University Press, 1987.

Zeman, J. "Moznosti trvale udrzitelneho vyvoje" [The possibilities of sustainable development]. *Narodni Hospodarstvi.* Vol. 47, No. 4–5, 1994.

Index